EVERYMAN, *I will go with thee,*

and be thy guide,

In thy most need to go by thy side

DYLAN THOMAS

Born at Swansea, 22nd October 1914.
Died in New York, 9th November 1953.
Buried at Laugharne, Wales.

Dylan Thomas
Miscellany Three

Poems and Stories

DENT: LONDON, MELBOURNE AND TORONTO
EVERYMAN'S LIBRARY

British Library Cataloguing in Publication Data

Thomas, Dylan
  Miscellany three.
  I. Title
  821'.9'12   PR6039.H52
  ISBN 0-460-01108-1

CONTENTS

I. POEMS

This Side of the Truth 3
To Others than You 5
Love in the Asylum 6
Unluckily for a Death 7
The Hunchback in the Park 9
Into her Lying Down Head 11
Paper and Sticks 14
A Winter's Tale 15
On a Wedding Anniversary 20
There was a Saviour 21
On the Marriage of a Virgin 23
When I Woke 24
Dawn Raid 25
Lie Still, Sleep Becalmed 26
Vision and Prayer 27
Holy Spring 39
A Pub Poem (untitled) 40

II. STORIES

The Fight 43
The Peaches 57
Old Garbo 76
After the Fair 91
The Enemies 96
Conversation about Christmas 102
How to be a Poet 109

Part I

POEMS

This Side of the Truth
(for Llewelyn)

This side of the truth,
You may not see, my son,
King of your blue eyes
In the blinding country of youth,
That all is undone,
Under the unminding skies,
Of innocence and guilt
Before you move to make
One gesture of the heart or head,
Is gathered and spilt
Into the winding dark
Like the dust of the dead.

Good and bad, two ways
Of moving about your death
By the grinding sea,
King of your heart in the blind days,
Blow away like breath,
Go crying through you and me
And the souls of all men
Into the innocent
Dark, and the guilty dark, and good
Death, and bad death, and then
In the last element
Fly like the stars' blood,

Like the sun's tears,
Like the moon's seed, rubbish
And fire, the flying rant
Of the sky, king of your six years.
And the wicked wish,
Down the beginning of plants
And animals and birds,

Water and light, the earth and sky,
Is cast before you move,
And all your deeds and words,
Each truth, each lie,
Die in unjudging love.

To Others than You

Friend by enemy I call you out.

You with a bad coin in your socket,
You my friend there with a winning air
Who palmed the lie on me when you looked
Brassily at my shyest secret,
Enticed with twinkling bits of the eye
Till the sweet tooth of my love bit dry,
Rasped at last, and I stumbled and sucked,
Whom now I conjure to stand as thief
In the memory worked by mirrors,
With unforgettably smiling act,
Quickness of hand in the velvet glove
And my whole heart under your hammer,
Were once such a creature, so gay and frank
A desireless familiar
I never thought to utter or think
While you displaced a truth in the air,

That though I loved them for their faults
As much as for their good,
My friends were enemies on stilts
With their heads in a cunning cloud.

Love in the Asylum

A stranger has come
To share my room in the house not right in the head,
A girl mad as birds

Bolting the night of the door with her arm her plume.
Strait in the mazed bed
She deludes the heaven-proof house with entering clouds

Yet she deludes with walking the nightmarish room,
At large as the dead,
Or rides the imagined oceans of the male wards.

She has come possessed
Who admits the delusive light through the bouncing wall,
Possessed by the skies

She sleeps in the narrow trough yet she walks the dust
Yet raves at her will
On the madhouse boards worn thin by my walking tears.

And taken by light in her arms at long and dear last
I may without fail
Suffer the first vision that set fire to the stars.

Unluckily for a death
Waiting with phoenix under
The pyre yet to be lighted of my sins and days,
And for the woman in shades
Saint carved and sensual among the scudding
Dead and gone, dedicate forever to my self
Though the brawl of the kiss has not occurred,
On the clay cold mouth, on the fire
Branded forehead, that could blind
Her constant, nor the winds of love broken wide
To the wind the choir and cloister
Of the wintry nunnery of the order of lust
Beneath my life, that sighs for the seducer's coming
In the sun strokes of summer,

Loving on this sea banged guilt
My holy lucky body
Under the cloud against love is caught and held and kissed
In the mill of the midst
Of the descending day, the dark our folly,
Cut to the still star in the order of the quick
But blessed by such heroic hosts in your every
Inch and glance that the wound
Is certain god, and the ceremony of souls
Is celebrated there, and communion between suns.
Never shall my self chant
About the saint in shades while the endless breviary
Turns of your preyed flesh, nor shall I shoo the bird below
    me:
The death biding two lie lonely.

I see the tigron in tears
In the androgynous dark,

His striped and noon maned tribe striding to holocaust,
The she mules bear their minotaurs,
The duck billed platypus broody in a milk of birds.
I see the wanting nun saint carved in a garb
Of shades, symbol of desire beyond my hours
And guilts, great crotch and giant
Continence. I see the unfired phoenix, herald
And heaven crier, arrow now of aspiring
And the renouncing of islands.
All love but for the full assemblage in flower
Of the living flesh is monstrous or immortal,
And the grave its daughters.

Love, my fate got luckily,
Teaches with no telling
That the phoenix' bid for heaven and the desire after
Death in the carved nunnery
Both shall fail if I bow not to your blessing
Nor walk in the cool of your mortal garden
With immortality at my side like Christ the sky.
This I know from the native
Tongue of your translating eyes. The young stars told me,
Hurling into beginning like Christ the child.
Lucklessly she must lie patient
And the vaulting bird be still. O my true love, hold me.
In your every inch and glance is the globe of genesis spun,
And the living earth your sons.

The Hunchback in the Park

The hunchback in the park
A solitary mister
Propped between trees and water
From the opening of the garden lock
That lets the trees and water enter
Until the Sunday sombre bell at dark

Eating bread from a newspaper
Drinking water from the chained cup
That the children filled with gravel
In the fountain basin where I sailed my ship
Slept at night in a dog kennel
But nobody chained him up.

Like the park birds he came early
Like the water he sat down
And Mister they called Hey mister
The truant boys from the town
Running when he had heard them clearly
On out of sound

Past lake and rockery
Laughing when he shook his paper
Hunchbacked in mockery
Through the loud zoo of the willow groves
Dodging the park keeper
With his stick that picked up leaves.

And the old dog sleeper
Alone between nurses and swans
While the boys among willows
Made the tigers jump out of their eyes
To roar on the rockery stones
And the groves were blue with sailors

Made all day until bell time
A woman figure without fault
Straight as a young elm
Straight and tall from his crooked bones
That she might stand in the night
After the locks and chains

All night in the unmade park
After the railings and shrubberies
The birds the grass the trees the lake
And the wild boys innocent as strawberries
Had followed the hunchback
To his kennel in the dark.

Into her Lying Down Head

(I)

Into her lying down head
His enemies entered bed,
Under the encumbered eyelid,
Through the rippled drum of the hair-buried ear;
And Noah's rekindled now unkind dove
Flew man-bearing there.
Last night in a raping wave
Whales unreined from the green grave
In fountains of origin gave up their love,
Along her innocence glided
Juan aflame and savagely young King Lear,
Queen Catherine howling bare
And Samson drowned in his hair,
The colossal intimacies of silent
Once seen strangers or shades on a stair;
There the dark blade and wanton sighing her down
To a haycock couch and the scythes of his arms
Rode and whistled a hundred times
Before the crowing morning climbed;
Man was the burning England she was sleep-walking, and
the enamouring island
Made her limbs blind by luminous charms,
Sleep to a newborn sleep in a swaddling loin-leaf stroked
and sang
And his runaway beloved childlike laid in the
acorned sand.

(II)

There where a numberless tongue
Wound their room with a male moan,
His faith around her flew undone
And darkness hung the walls with baskets of snakes,
A furnace-nostrilled column-membered

Super-or-near man
Resembling to her dulled sense
The thief of adolescence,
Early imaginary half remembered
Oceanic lover alone
Jealousy cannot forget for all her sakes,
Made his bad bed in her good
Night, and enjoyed as he would.
Crying, white gowned, from the middle moonlit stages
Out to the tiered and hearing tide,
Close and far she announced the theft of the heart
In the taken body at many ages,
Trespasser and broken bride
Celebrating at her side
All blood-signed assailings and vanished marriages in
which he had no lovely part
Nor could share, for his pride, to the least
Mutter and foul wingbeat of the solemnizing nightpriest
Her holy unholy hours with the always anonymous beast.

(III)

Two sand grains together in bed,
Head to heaven-circling head,
Singly lie with the whole wide shore,
The covering sea their nightfall with no names;
And out of every domed and soil-based shell
One voice in chains declaims
The female, deadly, and male
Libidinous betrayal,
Golden dissolving under the water veil.
A she bird sleeping brittle by
Her lover's wings that fold tomorrow's flight,
Within the nested treefork
Sings to the treading hawk
Carrion, paradise, chirrup my bright yolk.
A blade of grass longs with the meadow,
A stone lies lost and locked in the lark-high hill.

Open as to the air to the naked shadow
                    O she lies alone and still,
                    Innocent between two wars,
With the incestuous secret brother in the seconds to per-
                    petuate the stars,
          A man torn up mourns in the sole night.
And the second comers, the severers, the enemies from the
                    deep
Forgotten dark, rest their pulse and bury their dead in her
          faithless sleep.

Paper and Sticks

Paper and sticks and shovel and match
Why won't the news of the old world catch
And the fire in a temper start

Once I had a rich boy for myself
I loved his body and his navy blue wealth
And I lived in his purse and his heart

When in our bed I was tossing and turning
All I could see were his brown eyes burning
By the green of a one pound note

I talk to him as I clean the grate
O my dear it's never too late
To take me away as you whispered and wrote

I had a handsome and well-off boy
I'll share my money and we'll run for joy
With a bouncing and silver spooned kid

Sharp and shrill my silly tongue scratches
Words on the air as the fire catches
You never did and *he* never did.

A Winter's Tale

It is a winter's tale
That the snow blind twilight ferries over the lakes
And floating fields from the farm in the cup of the vales,
Gliding windless through the hand folded flakes,
The pale breath of cattle at the stealthy sail,

And the stars falling cold,
And the smell of hay in the snow, and the far owl
Warning among the folds, and the frozen hold
Flocked with the sheep white smoke of the farm house
    cowl
In the river wended vales where the tale was told.

Once when the world turned old
On a star of faith pure as the drifting bread,
As the food and flames of the snow, a man unrolled
The scrolls of fire that burned in his heart and head,
Torn and alone in a farm house in a fold

Of fields.   And burning then
In his firelit island ringed by the winged snow
And the dung hills white as wool and the hen
Roosts sleeping chill till the flame of the cock crow
Combs through the mantled yards and the morning men

Stumble out with their spades,
The cattle stirring, the mousing cat sleeping shy,
The puffed birds hopping and hunting, the milk maids
Gentle in their clogs over the fallen sky,
And all the woken farm at its white trades,

He knelt, he wept, he prayed,
By the spit and the black pot in the log bright light
And the cup and the cut bread in the dancing shade,

In the muffled house, in the quick of night,
At the point of love, forsaken and afraid.

He knelt on the cold stones,
He wept from the crest of grief, he prayed to the veiled sky
May his hunger go howling on bare white bones
Past the statues of the stables and the sky roofed sties
And the duck pond glass and the blinding byres alone.

Into the home of prayers
And fires where he should prowl down the cloud
Of his snow blind love and rush in the white lairs.
His naked need struck him howling and bowed
Though no sound flowed down the hand folded air

But only the wind strung
Hunger of birds in the fields of the bread of water, tossed
In high corn and the harvest melting on their tongues.
And his nameless need bound him burning and lost
When cold as snow he should run the wended vales among

The rivers mouthed in night,
And drown in the drifts of his need, and lie curled caught
In the always desiring centre of the white
Inhuman cradle and the bride bed forever sought
By the believer lost and the hurled outcast of light.

Deliver him, he cried,
By losing him all in love, and cast his need
Alone and naked in the engulfing bride,
Never to flourish in the fields of the white seed
Or flower under the time dying flesh astride.

Listen.   The minstrels sing
In the departed villages. The nightingale,
Dust in the buried wood, flies on the grains of her wings
And spells on the winds of the dead his winter's tale.
The voice of the dust of water from the withered spring

Is telling. The wizened
Stream with bells and baying water bounds. The dew rings
On the gristed leaves and the long gone glistening
Parish of snow. The carved mouths in the rock are wind
    swept strings.
Time sings through the intricately dead snow drop.
    Listen.

It was a hand or sound
In the long ago land that glided the dark door wide
And there outside on the bread of the ground
A she bird rose and rayed like a burning bride.
A she bird dawned, and her breast with snow and scarlet
    downed.

Look. And the dancers move
On the departed, snow bushed green, wanton in moon light
As a dust of pigeons. Exulting, the grave hooved
Horses, centaur dead, turn and tread the drenched white
Paddocks in the farms of birds. The dead oak walks for love

The carved limbs in the rock
Leap, as to trumpets. Calligraphy of the old
Leaves is dancing. Lines of age on the stones weave in a
    flock.
And the harp shaped voice of the water's dust plucks in a
    fold
Of fields. For love, the long ago she bird rises. Look.

And the wild wings were raised
Above her folded head, and the soft feathered voice
Was flying through the house as though the she bird
    praised
And all the elements of the slow fall rejoiced
That a man knelt alone in the cup of the vales,

In the mantle and calm,
By the spit and the black pot in the log bright light.
And the sky of birds in the plumed voice charmed
Him up and he ran like a wind after the kindling flight
Past the blind barns and byres of the windless farm.

In the poles of the year
When black birds died like priests in the cloaked hedge row
And over the cloth of counties the far hills rode near,
Under the one leaved trees ran a scarecrow of snow
And fast through the drifts of the thickets antlered like
    deer,

Rags and prayers down the knee-
Deep hillocks and loud on the numbed lakes,
All night lost and long wading in the wake of the she-
Bird through the times and lands and tribes of the slow
    flakes.
Listen and look where she sails the goose plucked sea,

The sky, the bird, the bride,
The cloud, the need, the planted stars, the joy beyond
The fields of seed and the time dying flesh astride,
The heavens, the heaven, the grave, the burning font.
In the far ago land the door of his death glided wide,

And the bird descended.
On a bread white hill over the cupped farm
And the lakes and floating fields and the river wended
Vales where he prayed to come to the last harm
And the home of prayers and fires, the tale ended.

The dancing perishes
On the white, no longer growing green, and, minstrel dead,
The singing breaks in the snow shoed villages of wishes
That once cut the figures of birds on the deep bread
And over the glazed lakes skated the shapes of fishes

Flying.   The rite is shorn
Of nightgale and centaur dead horse.   The springs wither
Back.   Lines of age sleep on the stones till trumpeting
   dawn.
Exultation lies down.   Time buries the spring weather
That belled and bounded with the fossil and the dew
   reborn.

For the bird lay bedded
In a choir of wings, as though she slept or died,
And the wings glided wide and he was hymned and
   wedded,
And through the thighs of the engulfing bride,
The woman breasted and the heaven headed

Bird, he was brought low,
Burning in the bride bed of love, in the whirl-
Pool at the wanting centre, in the folds
Of paradise, in the spun bud of the world.
And she rose with him flowering in her melting snow.

On a Wedding Anniversary

The sky is torn across
This ragged anniversary of two
Who moved for three years in tune
Down the long walks of their vows.

Now their love lies a loss
And Love and his patients roar on a chain;
From every true or crater
Carrying cloud, Death strikes their house.

Too late in the wrong rain
They come together whom their love parted:
The windows pour into their heart
And the doors burn in their brain.

There was a Saviour

There was a saviour
        Rarer than radium,
Commoner than water, crueller than truth;
        Children kept from the sun
        Assembled at his tongue
    To hear the golden note turn in a groove,
Prisoners of wishes locked their eyes
In the jails and studies of his keyless smiles.

        The voice of children says
        From a lost wilderness
There was calm to be done in his safe unrest,
        When hindering man hurt
        Man, animal, or bird
    We hid our fears in that murdering breath,
Silence, silence to do, when earth grew loud,
In lairs and asylums of the tremendous shout.

        There was glory to hear
        In the churches of his tears,
Under his downy arm you sighed as he struck,
        O you who could not cry
        On to the ground when a man died
    Put a tear for joy in the unearthly flood
And laid your cheek against a cloud-formed shell:
Now in the dark there is only yourself and myself.

        Two proud, blacked brothers cry,
        Winter-locked side by side,
To this inhospitable hollow year,
        O we who could not stir
        One lean sigh when we heard
    Greed on man beating near and fire neighbour

But wailed and nested in the sky-blue wall
Now break a giant tear for the little known fall,

   For the drooping of homes
      That did not nurse our bones,
   Brave deaths of only ones but never found,
      Now see, alone in us,
      Our own true strangers' dust
   Ride through the doors of our unentered house.
Exiled in us we arouse the soft,
Unclenched, armless, silk and rough love that breaks all
   rocks.

On the Marriage of a Virgin

Waking alone in a multitude of loves when morning's light
Surprised in the opening of her nightlong eyes
His golden yesterday asleep upon the iris
And this day's sun leapt up the sky out of her thighs
Was miraculous virginity old as loaves and fishes,
Though the moment of a miracle is unending lightning
And the shipyards of Galilee's footprints hide a navy of
    doves.

No longer will the vibrations of the sun desire on
Her deepsea pillow where once she married alone,
Her heart all ears and eyes, lips catching the avalanche
Of the golden ghost who ringed with his streams her
    mercury bone,
Who under the lids of her windows hoisted his golden
    luggage,
For a man sleeps where fire leapt down and she learns
    through his arm
That other sun, the jealous coursing of the unrivalled
    blood.

When I Woke

When I woke, the town spoke.
Birds and clocks and cross bells
Dinned aside the coiling crowd,
The reptile profligates in a flame,
Spoilers and pokers of sleep,
The next-door sea dispelled
Frogs and satans and woman-luck,
While a man outside with a billhook,
Up to his head in his blood,
Cutting the morning off,
The warm-veined double of Time
And his scarving beard from a book,
Slashed down the last snake as though
It were a wand or subtle bough,
Its tongue peeled in the wrap of a leaf.

Every morning I make,
God in bed, good and bad,
After a water-face walk,
The death-stagged scatter-breath
Mammoth and sparrowfall
Everybody's earth.
Where birds ride like leaves and boats like ducks
I heard, this morning, waking,
Crossly out of the town noises
A voice in the erected air,
No prophet-progeny of mine,
Cry my sea town was breaking.
No Time, spoke the clocks, no God, rang the bells,
I drew the white sheet over the islands
And the coins on my eyelids sang like shells.

Among those Killed in the Dawn Raid was a Man Aged a Hundred

When the morning was waking over the war
He put on his clothes and stepped out and he died,
The locks yawned loose and a blast blew them wide,
He dropped where he loved on the burst pavement stone
And the funeral grains of the slaughtered floor.
Tell his street on its back he stopped a sun
And the craters of his eyes grew springshoots and fire
When all the keys shot from the locks, and rang.
Dig no more for the chains of his grey-haired heart.
The heavenly ambulance drawn by a wound
Assembling waits for the spade's ring on the cage.
O keep his bones away from that common cart,
The morning is flying on the wings of his age
And a hundred storks perch on the sun's right hand.

Lie Still, Sleep Becalmed

Lie still, sleep becalmed, sufferer with the wound
In the throat, burning and turning. All night afloat
On the silent sea we have heard the sound
That came from the wound wrapped in the salt sheet.

Under the mile off moon we trembled listening
To the sea sound flowing like blood from the loud wound
And when the salt sheet broke in a storm of singing
The voices of all the drowned swam on the wind.

Open a pathway through the slow sad sail,
Throw wide to the wind the gates of the wandering boat
For my voyage to begin to the end of my wound,
We heard the sea sound sing, we saw the salt sheet tell.
Lie still, sleep becalmed, hide the mouth in the throat,
Or we shall obey, and ride with you through the drowned.

Vision and Prayer

(1)
Who
Are you
Who is born
In the next room
So loud to my own
That I can hear the womb
Opening and the dark run
Over the ghost and the dropped son
Behind the wall thin as a wren's bone?
In the birth bloody room unknown
To the burn and turn of time
And the heart print of man
Bows no baptism
But dark alone
Blessing on
The wild
Child.

I

Must lie

Still as stone

By the wren bone

Wall hearing the moan

Of the mother hidden

And the shadowed head of pain

Casting tomorrow like a thorn

And the midwives of miracle sing

Until the turbulent new born

Burns me his name and his flame

And the winged wall is torn

By his torrid crown

And the dark thrown

From his loin

To bright

Light.

When
The wren
Bone writhes down
And the first dawn
Furied by his stream
Swarms on the kingdom come
Of the dazzler of heaven
And the splashed mothering maiden
Who bore him with a bonfire in
His mouth and rocked him like a storm
I shall run lost in sudden
Terror and shining from
The once hooded room
Crying in vain
In the caldron
Of his
Kiss

In

The spin

Of the sun

In the spuming

Cyclone of his wing

For I lost was who am

Crying at the man drenched throne

In the first fury of his stream

And the lightnings of adoration

Back to black silence melt and mourn

For I was lost who have come

To dumbfounding haven

And the finding one

And the high noon

Of his wound

Blinds my

Cry.

There
Crouched bare
In   the   shrine
Of his blazing
Breast I shall waken
To the judge blown bedlam
Of the uncaged sea bottom
The cloud climb of the exhaling tomb
And the bidden dust upsailing
With his flame in every grain.
O spiral of ascension
From the vultured urn
Of the morning
Of man when
The land
And

The
Born sea
Praised the sun
The finding one
And upright Adam
Sang upon origin!
O the wings of the children!
The woundward flight of the ancient
Young from the canyons of oblivion!
The sky stride of the always slain
In battle! the happening
Of saints to their vision!
The world winding home!
And the whole pain
Flows open
And I
Die.

In the name of the lost who glory in

The   swinish   plains   of   carrion

Under   the   burial   song

Of the birds of burden

Heavy with the drowned

And the green dust

And bearing

The ghost

From

The ground

Like pollen

On the black plume

And the beak of slime

I   pray   though   I   belong

Not   wholly   to   that   lamenting

Brethren for joy has moved within

The inmost marrow of my heart bone

That he who learns now the sun and moon

Of his mother's milk may return

Before the lips blaze and bloom

To the birth bloody room

Behind the wall's wren

Bone and be dumb

And the womb

That bore

For

All men

Theadored

Infant light or

The dazzling prison

Yawn to his upcoming.

In the name of the wanton

Lost on the unchristened mountain

In the centre of dark I pray him

Then he let the dead lie though they moan

For his briared hands to hoist them

To the shrine of his world's wound

And the blood drop's garden

E n d u r e t h e s t o n e

Blind host to sleep

I n t h e d a r k

A n d d e e p

Rock

A w a k e

No heart bone

But let it break

On the mountain crown

U n b i d d e n b y t h e s u n

And the beating dust be blown

Down to the river rooting plain

Under the night forever falling.

Forever falling night is a known
Star and country to the legion
Of sleepers whose tongue I toll
To   mourn   his   deluging
Light through sea and soil
And we have come
To know all
P l a c e s
Ways
M a z e s
P a s s a g e s
Quarters and graves
Of   the   endless   fall.
Now common lazarus
Of the charting sleepers prays
Never to awake and arise
For the country of death is the heart's size

And the star of the lost the shape of the eyes.

In   the   name   of   the   fatherless

In   the   name   of   the   unborn

A n d   t h e   u n d e s i r e r s

Of midwiving morning's

Hands or instruments

O in the name

Of no one

Now or

No

One   to

B e   I   p r a y

May   the   crimson

Sun spin a grave grey

And   the   colour   of   clay

Stream   upon   his   martyrdom

In   the   interpreted   evening

And the known dark of the earth amen.

I turn the corner of prayer and burn
In a blessing of the sudden
Sun. In the name of the damned
I would turn back and run
To the hidden land
But the loud sun
Christens down
The sky.
I
Am found.
O let him
Scald me and drown
Me in his world's wound.
His lightning answers my
Cry. My voice burns in his hand.
Now I am lost in the blinding
One. The sun roars at the prayer's end.

Holy Spring

O
Out of a bed of love
When that immortal hospital made one more move to
    soothe
            The cureless counted body,
                    And ruin and his causes
Over the barbed and shooting sea assumed an army
            And swept into our wounds and houses,
I climb to greet the war in which I have no heart but only
            That one dark I owe my light,
Call for confessor and wiser mirror but there is none
            To glow after the god stoning night
And I am struck as lonely as a holy maker by the sun.

No
Praise that the spring time is all
Gabriel and radiant shrubbery as the morning grows joyful
            Out of the woebegone pyre
And the multitude's sultry tear turns cool on the weeping
    wall,
            My arising prodigal
Sun the father his quiver full of the infants of pure fire,
            But blessed be hail and upheaval
That uncalm still it is sure alone to stand and sing
            Alone in the husk of man's home
And the mother and toppling house of the holy spring,
            If only for a last time.

A pub poem
Untitled

Sooner than you can water milk or cry Amen
Darkness comes, psalming, over Cards again;
Some lights go on; some men go out; some men slip in;
Some girls lie down, calling the beer-brown bulls to sin
And boom among their fishy fields; some elders stand
With thermoses and telescopes and spy the sand
Where farmers plough by night and sailors rock and rise,
Tattooed with texts, between the Atlantic thighs
Of Mrs Rosser Tea and little Nell the Knock;
One pulls out *Pam in Paris* from his money sock;
One from the mothy darkness of his black back house
Drinks vinegar and paraffin and blinds a mouse;
One reads his cheque book in the dark and eats fish-heads;
One creeps into the Cross Inn and fouls the beds;
One in the rubbered hedges rolls with a bald Liz
Who's old enough to be his mother (and she is);
Customers in the snugbar by the gobgreen logs
Tell other customers what they do with dogs;
The chemist is performing an unnatural act
In the organ loft; and the lavatory is packed.

Part II

STORIES

THE FIGHT

I was standing at the end of the lower playground and annoying Mr Samuels, who lived in the house just below the high railings. Mr Samuels complained once a week that boys from the school threw apples and stones and balls through his bedroom window. He sat in a deck chair in a small square of trim garden and tried to read the newspaper. I was only a few yards from him. I was staring him out. He pretended not to notice me, but I knew he knew I was standing there rudely and quietly. Every now and then he peeped at me from behind his newspaper, saw me still and serious and alone, with my eyes on his. As soon as he lost his temper I was going to go home. Already I was late for dinner. I had almost beaten him, the newspaper was trembling, he was breathing heavily, when a strange boy, whom I had not heard approach, pushed me down the bank.

I threw a stone at his face. He took off his spectacles, put them in his coat pocket, took off his coat, hung it neatly on the railings, and attacked. Turning round as we wrestled on the top of the bank, I saw that Mr Samuels had folded his newspaper on the deck chair and was standing up to watch us. It was a mistake to turn round. The strange boy rabbit-punched me twice. Mr Samuels hopped with excitement as I fell against the railings. I was down in the dust, hot and scratched and biting, then up and dancing, and I butted the boy in the belly and we tumbled in a heap. I saw through a closing eye that his nose was bleeding. I hit his nose. He tore at my collar and spun me round by the hair.

'Come on! come on!' I heard Mr Samuels cry.

We both turned towards him. He was shaking his fists and dodging about in the garden. He stopped then, and coughed, and set his panama straight, and avoided our eyes, and turned his back and walked slowly to the deck chair.

We both threw gravel at him.

'I'll give him "Come on!"' the boy said, as we ran along the playground away from the shouts of Mr Samuels and down the steps on to the hill.

We walked home together. I admired his bloody nose. He said that my eye was like a poached egg, only black.

'I've never seen such a lot of blood,' I said.

He said I had the best black eye in Wales, perhaps it was the best black eye in Europe; he bet Tunney never had a black eye like that.

'And there's blood all over your shirt.'

'Sometimes I bleed in dollops,' he said.

On Walter's Road we passed a group of high school girls, and I cocked my cap and hoped my eye was as big as a blue-bag, and he walked with his coat flung open to show the bloodstains.

I was a hooligan all during dinner, and a bully, and as bad as a boy from the Sandbanks, and I should have more respect, and I sat silently, like Tunney, over the sago pudding. That afternoon I went to school with an eye-shade on. If I had had a black silk sling I would have been as gay and desperate as the wounded captain in the book that my sister used to read, and that I read under the bedclothes at night, secretly with a flash-lamp.

On the road, a boy from an inferior school, where the parents did not have to pay anything, called me 'One eye!' in a harsh, adult voice. I took no notice, but walked along whistling, my good eye on the summer clouds sailing, beyond insult, above Terrace Road.

The mathematics master said; 'I see that Mr Thomas at the back of the class has been straining his eyesight. But it isn't over his homework, is it, gentlemen?'

Gilbert Rees, next to me, laughed loudest.

'I'll break your leg after school!' I said.

He'd hobble, howling, up to the head master's study. A deep hush in the school. A message on a plate brought by the porter. 'The head master's compliments, sir, and will you come at once?' 'How did you happen to break this boy's leg?' 'Oh! damn and bottom, the agony!' cried Gilbert Rees. 'Just a little twist,' I would say. 'I don't know my own strength. I apologize. But there's nothing to worry about. Let me set the leg, sir.' A rapid manipulation, the click of a bone. 'Doctor Thomas, sir, at your service.' Mrs Rees was on her knees. 'How can I thank you?' 'It's nothing at all, dear lady. Wash his ears every morning. Throw away his rulers. Pour his red and green inks down the sink.'

In Mr Trotter's drawing class we drew naked girls inaccurately on sheets of paper under our drawings of a vase and passed them along under the desks. Some of the drawings were detailed strangely others were tailed off like mermaids. Gilbert Rees drew the vase only.

'Sleep with your wife, sir?'

'What did you say?'

'Lend me a knife, sir?'

'What would you do if you had a million pounds?'

'I'd buy a Bugatti and a Rolls and a Bentley and I'd go two hundred miles an hour on Pendine sands.'

'I'd buy a harem and keep the girls in the gym.'

'I'd buy a house like Mrs Cotmore-Richard's, twice as big as hers, and a cricket field and a football field and a proper garage with mechanics and a lift.'

'And a lavatory as big as, as big as the Melba pavilion, with plush seats and a golden chain and . . .'

'And I'd smoke cigarettes with real gold tips, better than Morris's Blue Book.'

'I'd buy all the railway trains, and only 4A could travel in them.'

'And not Gilbert Rees either.'

'What's the longest you've been?'

'I went to Edinburgh.'

'My father went to Salonika in the War.'

'Where's that, Cyril?'

'Cyril, tell us about Mrs Pussie Edwards in Hanover Street.'

'Well, my brother says he can do anything.'

I drew a wild guess below the waist, and wrote Pussie Edwards in small letters at the foot of the page.

'Cave!'

'Hide your drawings.'

'I bet you a greyhound can go faster than a horse.'

Everybody liked the drawing class, except Mr Trotter.

In the evening, before calling on my new friend, I sat in my bedroom by the boiler and read through my exercise-books full of poems. There were Danger Don'ts on the backs. On my bedroom walls were pictures of Shakespeare, Walter de la Mare torn from my father's Christmas *Bookman*, Robert Browning, Stacy Aumonier, Rupert Brooke, a bearded man who I had discovered was Whittier, Watt's 'Hope', and a Sunday school certificate I was ashamed to want to pull down. A poem I had had printed in the 'Wales Day by Day' column of the *Western Mail* was pasted on the mirror to make me blush, but the shame of the poem had died. Across the poem I had written, with a stolen quill and in flourishes: 'Homer Nods'. I was always waiting for the opportunity to bring someone into my bedroom – 'Come into my den; excuse the untidiness; take a chair. No! not that one, it's broken!' – and force him to see the poem accidentally. 'I put it there to make me blush.' But nobody ever came in except my mother.

Walking to his house in the early dusk through solid, deserted professional avenues lined with trees, I recited pieces of my poems and heard my voice, like a stranger's voice in Park Drive accompanied by the tap-tapping of nailed boots, rise very thinly up through the respectable autumn evening.

'My mind is fashioned
In the ways of intertissue;
    Veiled and passioned
    Are the thoughts that issue
From its well of furtive lust
Raptured by the devil's dust.'

If I looked through a window on to the road, I would see
a scarlet-capped boy with big boots striding down the
middle, and would wonder who it could be. If I were a
young girl watching, my face like Mona Lisa's, my coal-
black hair coiled in earphones, I'd see beneath the 'Boys'
Department' suit a manly body with hair and sun tan, and
call him and ask, 'Will you have tea or cocktails?' and hear
his voice reciting the *Grass Blade's Psalm* in the half-dark
of the heavily curtained and coloured drawing-room hung
about with famous reproductions and glowing with books
and wine bottles:

'The frost has lain,
Frost that is dark with flowered slain,
    Fragilely strewn
    With patches of illuminated moon,
About my lonely head in flagged unlovely red.

'The frost has spake,
Frost secretive and thrilled in silent flake,
    With unseen lips of blue
    Glass in the glaze stars threw,
    Only to my ears, has spake in visionary tears.

'The frost has known,
From scattered conclave by the few winds blown,
    That the lone genius in my roots,
    Bare down there in a jungle of fruits,
Has planted a green year, for praise in the heart of my
    upgrowing days.

'The frost has filled
My heart with longing that the night's sleeve spilled,
Frost of celestial vapour fraught,
Frost that the columns of unfallen snow have sought,
With desire for the fields of space hovering about my single
place.'

'Look! there's a strange boy, walking alone like a prince.'
'No, no, like a wolf! Look at his long stride!' Sketty
church was shaking its bells for me.

'When I am strewn low
And all my ashes are
Dust in a dumb provoking show
Of minatory star . . .'

I recited. A young man and woman, arm in arm, suddenly
appeared from a black lane between houses. I changed my
recitation into a tune and hummed past them. They would
be tittering together now, with their horrid bodies close.
Cissy, moony, long hair. I whistled hard and loud, kicked a
tradesmen's entrance, and glanced back over my shoulder. The couple were gone. Here's a kick at 'The Elms'.
'Where are the bleedy elms, mister?' Here's a handful of
gravel, Mrs 'The Croft', right at your window. One night I
would paint 'Bum' all over the front gate of 'Kia-ora'.

A woman stood on 'Lyndhurst' steps with a hissing
pom, and, stuffing my cap in my pocket, I was off down the
road; and there was Dan's house, 'Warmley', with music
coming loudly out of it.

He was a composer and a poet too; he had written seven
historical novels before he was twelve, and he played the
piano and the violin; his mother made wool pictures, his
brother was a clerk at the docks and syncopated, his aunt
kept a preparatory school on the first floor, and his father
wrote music for the organ. All this he had told me as we
walked home bleeding, strutting by the gym-frocks waving
to boys in the trams.

My new friend's mother answered the door with a ball of wool in her hand. Dan, in the upstairs drawing-room, heard my arrival and played the piano faster.

'I didn't hear you come in,' he said when I found him. He finished on a grand chord, stretching all his fingers.

The room was splendidly untidy, full of wool and paper and open cupboards stacked with things you could never find; all the expensive furniture had been kicked; a waist-coat hung on the chandelier. I thought I could live for ever in that room, writing and fighting and spilling ink, having my friends for picnics there after midnight with Waller's rum-and-butter and charlottes russes from Eynon's, and Cydrax and Vino.

He showed me his books and his seven novels. All the novels were about battles, sieges, and kings. 'Just early stuff,' he said.

He let me take out his violin and make a cat noise.

We sat on a sofa in the window and talked as though we had always known each other. Would the 'Swans' beat the 'Spurs'? When could girls have babies? Was Arnott's average last year better than Clay's?

'That's my father outside there on the road,' he said, 'the tall one waving his arms.'

Two men were talking on the tram lines. Mr Jenkyn looked as if he were trying to swim down Eversley Road, he breast-stroked the air and beat on the ground with his feet, and then he limped and raised one shoulder higher than the other.

'Perhaps he's describing a fight,' I said.

'Or telling Mr Morris a story about cripples,' said Dan. 'Can you play the piano?'

'I can do chords, but not tunes,' I said.

We played a duet with crossed hands.

'Now who's that sonata by?'

We made a Dr Percy, who was the greatest composer for four hands in the world, and I was Paul America, the pianist, and Dan was Winter Vaux.

I read him an exercise-book full of poems. He listened wisely, like a boy aged a hundred, his head on one side and his spectacles shaking on his swollen nose. 'This is called *Warp*,' I said:

> 'Like suns red from running tears,
> Five suns in the glass,
> Together, separate yet, yet separately round,
> Red perhaps, but the glass is as pale as grass,
> Glide, without sound.
> In unity, five tears lid-awake, suns yet, but salt,
> Five inscrutable spears in the head,
> Each sun but an agony,
> Twist perhaps, pain bled of hate,
> Five into one, the one made of five into one, early
> Suns distorted to late.
> All of them now, madly and desolate,
> Spun with the cloth of the five, run
> Widely and foaming, wildly and desolate,
> Shoot through and dive. One of the five is the sun.'

The noise of the trams past the house clattered away as far as the sea or farther, into the dredgered bay. Nobody had ever listened like that before. The school had vanished, leaving on Mount Pleasant hill a deep hole that smelt of cloakrooms and locker mice, and 'Warmley' shone in the dark of a town I did not know. In the still room, that had never been strange to me, sitting in heaps of coloured wool, swollen-nosed and one-eyed, we acknowledged our gifts. The future spread out beyond the window, over Singleton Park crowded with lovers messing about, and into smoky London paved with poems.

Mrs Jenkyn peered round the door and switched the light on. 'There, that's more homely,' she said. 'You aren't cats.'

The future went out with the light, and we played a thumping piece by Dr Percy – 'Have you ever heard anything so beautiful? Louder, louder, America!' said Dan.

'Leave a bit of bass for me,' I said – until the next-door wall was rapped.

'That's the Careys. Mr Carey's a Cape Horner,' Dan said.

We played him one harsh, whaling piece before Mrs Jenkyn, with wool and needles, ran upstairs.

When she had gonè, Dan said: 'Why is a man always ashamed of his mother?'

'Perhaps he isn't when he is older,' I said, but I doubted it. The week before I was walking down High Street with three boys after school, and I saw my mother with a Mrs Partridge outside the Kardomah. I knew she would stop me in front of the others and say, 'Now you be home early for tea,' and I wanted High Street to open and suck me down. I loved her and disowned her. 'Let's cross over,' I said, 'there's some sailors' boots in Griffith's window.' But there was only a dummy with a golf suit on, and a roll of tweed.

'Supper isn't for half an hour yet. What shall we do?'

'Let's see who can hold up that chair the longest,' I said.

'No, let's edit a paper: you do the literature, I'll do the music.'

'What shall we call it, then?'

He wrote, '*The* ———, edited by D. Jenkyn and D. Thomas,' on the back of a hat-box from under the sofa. The rhythm was better with D. Thomas and D. Jenkyn, but it was his house.

'What about *The Maestersingers?*'

'No, that's too musical,' I said.

'*The Warmley Magazine?*'

'No,' I said, 'I live in "Glanrhyd".'

After the hat-box was covered, we wrote.

'*The Thunderer*, edited by D. Jenkyn Thomas', in chalk on a piece of cardboard and pinned it on the wall.

'Would you like to see our maid's bedroom?' asked Dan. We whispered up to the attic.

'What's her name?'

'Hilda.'

'Is she young?'

'No, she's twenty or thirty.'

Her bed was untidy. 'My mother says you can always smell a maid.' We smelled the sheets. 'I can't smell anything.'

In her brass-bound box was a framed photograph of a young man wearing plus-fours.

'That's her boy.'

'Let's give him a moustache.'

Somebody moved downstairs, a voice called, 'Supper now!' and we hurried out, leaving the box open. 'One night we'll hide under her bed,' Dan said as we opened the dining-room door.

Mr Jenkyn, Mrs Jenkyn, Dan's aunt, and a Reverend Bevan and Mrs Bevan were seated at the table.

Mr Bevan said grace. When he stood up, it was just as though he were still sitting down, he was so short. Bless our repast this evening,' he said, as though he didn't like the food at all. But once 'Amen' was over, he went at the cold meat like a dog.

Mrs Bevan didn't look all there. She stared at the table-cloth and made hesitant movements with her knife and fork. She appeared to be wondering which to cut up first, the meat or the cloth.

Dan and I stared at her with delight; he kicked me under the table and I spilt the salt. In the commotion I managed to put some vinegar on his bread.

Mrs Jenkyn said, while everyone except Mr Bevan was watching Mrs Bevan moving her knife slowly along the edge of her plate: 'I do hope you like cold lamb.'

Mrs Bevan smiled at her, assured, and began to eat. She was grey-haired and grey-faced. Perhaps she was grey all over. I tried to undress her, but my mind grew frightened when it came to her short flannel petticoat and navy bloomers to the knees. I couldn't even dare unbutton her tall boots to see how grey her legs were. She looked up from her plate and gave me a wicked smile.

Blushing, I turned to answer Mr Jenkyn, who was asking me how old I was. I told him, but added one year. Why did I lie then? I wondered. If I lost my cap and found it in my bedroom, and my mother asked me where I had found it, I would say, 'In the attic,' or 'Under the hall stand.' It was exciting to have to keep wary all the time in case I contradicted myself, to make up the story of a film I pretended to have seen and put Jack Holt in Richard Dix's place.

'Fifteen and three-quarters,' said Mr Jenkyn. 'that's a very exact age. I see we have a mathematician with us. Now see if he can do this little sum.'

He finished his supper and laid out matches on the plate.

'That's an old one,' Dad, Dan said.

'Oh, I'd like to see it very much,' I said in my best voice. I wanted to come to the house again. This was better than home, and there was a woman off her head, too.'

When I failed to place the matches rightly, Mr Jenkyn showed me how it was done, and, still not understanding, I thanked him and asked him for another one. It was almost as good being a hypocrite as being a liar; it made you warm and shameful.

'What were you talking to Mr Morris about in the street, Dad?' asked Dan. 'We saw you from upstairs.'

'I was telling him how the Swansea and District Male Voice did the *Messiah*, that's all. Why do you ask?'

Mr Bevan couldn't eat any more, he was full. For the first time since supper began, he looked round the table. He didn't seem to like what he saw. 'How are studies progressing, Daniel?'

'Listen to Mr Bevan, Dan, he's asking you a question.'

'Oh, so so.'

'So so?'

'I mean they're going very well, thank you, Mr Bevan.'

'Young people should attempt to say what they mean.'

Mrs Bevan giggled, and asked for more meat. 'More meat,' she said.

'And you, young man, have you a mathematical bent?'

'No, sir,' I said, 'I like English.'

'He's a poet,' said Dan, and looked uncomfortable.

'A brother poet,' Mr Bevan corrected, showing his teeth.

'Mr Bevan has published books,' said Mr Jenkyn. '*Proserpine, Psyche*——'

'*Orpheus*,' said Mr Bevan sharply.

'And *Orpheus*. You must show Mr Bevan some of your verses.'

'I haven't got anything with me, Mr Jenkyn.'

'A poet,' said Mr Bevan, 'should carry his verses in his head.'

'I remember them all right,' I said.

'Recite me your latest one; I'm always very interested.'

'What a gathering,' Mrs Jenkyn said, 'poets, musicians, preachers. We only want a painter now, don't we?'

'I don't think you'll like the very latest one,' I said.

'Perhaps,' said Mr Bevan, smiling, 'I am the best judge of that.'

'Frivolous is my hate,' I said, wanting to die, watching Mr Bevan's teeth.

> 'Singed with bestial remorse
> Of unfulfilment of desired force,
> And lust of tearing late;
>
> 'Now could I raise
> Her dead, dark body to my own
> And hear the joyous rustle of her bone
> And in her eyes see deathly blaze;
>
> 'Now could I wake
> To passion after death, and taste
> The rapture of her hating, tear the waste
> Of body. Break, her dead, dark body, break.'

Dan kicked my shins in the silence before Mr Bevan said: 'The influence is obvious, of course. "Break, break, break, on thy cold, grey stones, O sea."'

'Hubert knows Tennyson backwards,' said Mrs Bevan, 'backwards.'

'Can we go upstairs now?' Dan asked.

'No annoying Mr Carey then.'

And we shut the door softly behind us and ran upstairs with our hands over our mouths.

'Damn! damn! damn!' said Dan. 'Did you see the reverend's face?'

We imitated him up and down the room, and had a short fight on the carpet. Dan's nose began to bleed again. 'That's nothing, it'll stop in a minute. I can bleed when I like.'

'Tell me about Mrs Bevan. Is she mad?'

'She's terribly mad, she doesn't know who she is. She tried to throw herself out of the window but he didn't take any notice, so she came up to our house and told mother all about it.'

Mrs Bevan knocked and walked in. 'I hope I'm not interrupting you.'

'No, of course not, Mrs Bevan.'

'I wanted a little change of air,' she said. She sat down in the wool on the sofa by the window.

'Isn't it a close night?' said Dan. 'Would you like the window open?'

She looked at the window.

'I can easily open it for you,' Dan said, and winked at me.

'Let me open it for you, Mrs Bevan,' I said.

'It's good to have the window open.'

'And this is a nice high window too.'

'Plenty of air from the sea.'

'Let it be, dear,' she said. 'I'll just sit here and wait for my husband.'

She played with the balls of wool, picked up a needle and tapped it gently on the palm of her hand.

'Is Mr Bevan going to be long?'

'I'll just sit and wait for my husband,' she said.

We talked to her some more about windows, but she only smiled and undid the wool, and once she put the blunt end of the long needle in her ear. Soon we grew tired of watching her, and Dan played the piano – 'My twentieth sonata,' he said, 'this one is *Homage to Beethoven*' – and at half-past nine I had to go home.

I said good night to Mrs Bevan, who waved the needle and bowed sitting down, and Mr Bevan downstairs gave me his cold hand to shake, and Mr and Mrs Jenkyn told me to come again, and the quiet aunt gave me a Mars bar.

'I'll send you a bit of the way,' said Dan.

Outside, on the pavement, in the warm night, we looked up at the lighted drawing-room window. It was the only light in the road.

'Look! there she is!'

Mrs Bevan's face was pressed against the glass, her hook nose flattened, her lips pressed tight, and we ran all the way down Eversley Road in case she jumped.

At the corner, Dan said: 'I must leave you now, I've got to finish a string trio to-night.'

'I'm working on a long poem,' I said, 'about the princes of Wales and the wizards and everybody.'

We both went home to bed.

THE PEACHES

The grass-green cart, with 'J. Jones, Gorsehill' painted shakily on it, stopped in the cobblestone passage between 'The Hare's Foot' and 'The Pure Drop'. It was late on an April evening. Uncle Jim, in his black market suit with a stiff white shirt and no collar, loud new boots, and a plaid cap, creaked and climbed down. He dragged out a thick wicker basket from a heap of straw in the corner of the cart and swung it over his shoulder. I heard a squeal from the basket and saw the tip of a pink tail curling out as Uncle Jim opened the public door of 'The Pure Drop'.

'I won't be two minutes,' he said to me. The bar was full; two fat women in bright dresses sat near the door, one with a small dark child on her knee; they saw Uncle Jim and nudged up on the bench.

'I'll be out straight away,' he said fiercely, as though I had contradicted him, 'you stay there quiet.'

The woman without the child raised up her hands. 'Oh, Mr Jones,' she said in a high laughing voice. She shook like a jelly.

Then the door closed and the voices were muffled.

I sat alone on the shaft of the cart in the narrow passage, staring through a side window of 'The Hare's Foot'. A stained blind was drawn half over it. I could see into half of a smoky, secret room, where four men were playing cards. One man was huge and swarthy, with a handlebar moustache and a love-curl on his forehead; seated by his side was a thin, bald, pale old man with his cheeks in his mouth; the faces of the other two were in shadow. They all drank out of brown pint tankards and never spoke, laying the cards down with a smack, scraping at their match-boxes, puffing at their pipes, swallowing unhappily, ringing the brass bell, ordering more, by a sign of the fingers, from a sour woman with a flowered blouse and a man's cap.

The passage grew dark too suddenly, the walls crowded in, and the roofs crouched down. To me, staring timidly there in the dark passage in a strange town, the swarthy man appeared like a giant in a cage surrounded by clouds, and the bald old man withered into a black hump with a white top; two white hands darted out of the corner with invisible cards. A man with spring-heeled boots and a two-edged knife might be bouncing towards me from Union Street.

I called, 'Uncle Jim, Uncle Jim,' softly so that he should not hear.

I began to whistle between my teeth, but when I stopped I thought the sound went hissing on behind me. I climbed down from the shaft and stepped close to the half-blind window; a hand clawed up the pane to the tassel of the blind; in the little, packed space between me on the cobbles and the card-players at the table, I could not tell which side of the glass was the hand that dragged the blind down slowly. I was cut from the night by a stained square. A story I had made in the warm, safe island of my bed, with sleepy midnight Swansea flowing and rolling round outside the house, came blowing down to me then with a noise on the cobbles. I remembered the demon in the story, with his wings and hooks, who clung like a bat to my hair as I battled up and down Wales after a tall, wise, golden, royal girl from Swansea convent. I tried to remember her true name, her proper, long, black-stockinged legs, her giggle and paper curls, but the hooked wings tore at me and the colour of her hair and eyes faded and vanished like the grass-green of the cart that was a dark, grey mountain now standing between the passage walls.

And all this time the old, broad, patient, nameless mare stood without stirring, not stamping once on the cobbles or shaking her reins. I called her a good girl and stood on tip-toe to try to stroke her ears as the door of 'The Pure Drop' swung open and the warm lamplight from the bar dazzled me and burned my story up. I felt frightened no longer, only angry and hungry. The two fat women near the door giggled 'Good night, Mr Jones' out of the rich noise and the comfortable smells. The child lay curled asleep under the bench. Uncle Jim kissed the two women on the lips.

'Good night.'

'Good night.'

'Good night.'

Then the passage was dark again.

He backed the mare into Union Street, lurching against her side, cursing her patience and patting her nose, and we both climbed into the cart.

'There are too many drunken gipsies,' he said as we rolled and rattled through the flickering lamp-lit town.

He sang hymns all the way to Gorsehill in an affectionate bass voice, and conducted the wind with his whip. He did not need to touch the reins. Once on the rough road, between hedges twisting out to twig the mare by the bridle and poke our caps, we stopped at a whispered 'Whoa', for uncle to light his pipe and set the darkness on fire and show his long, red, drunken fox's face to me, with its bristling side-bushes and wet, sensitive nose. A white house with a light in one bedroom window shone in a field on a short hill beyond the road.

Uncle whispered, 'Easy, easy, girl,' to the mare, though she was standing calmly, and said to me over his shoulder in a suddenly loud voice: 'A hangman lived there.'

He stamped on the shaft, and we rattled on through a cutting wind. Uncle shivered, pulling down his cap to hide his ears; but the mare was like a clumsy statue trotting, and all the demons of my stories, if they trotted by her side or crowded together and grinned into her eyes, would not make her shake her head or hurry.

'I wish he'd have hung Mrs Jesus,' uncle said.

Between hymns he cursed the mare in Welsh. The white house was left behind, the light and the hill were swallowed up.

'Nobody lives there now,' he said.

We drove into the farm-yard of Gorsehill, where the cobbles rang and the black, empty stables took up the ringing and hollowed it so that we drew up in a hollow circle of darkness and the mare was a hollow animal and nothing lived in the hollow house at the end of the yard but two sticks with faces scooped out of turnips.

'You run and see Annie,' said uncle. 'There'll be hot broth and potatoes.'

He led the hollow, shappy statue towards the stable; clop, clop to the mice-house. I heard locks rattle as I ran to the farm-house door.

The front of the house was the single side of a black shell, and the arched door was the listening ear. I pushed the door open and walked into the passage out of the wind. I might have been walking into the hollow night and the wind, passing through a tall vertical shell on an inland sea-shore. Then a door at the end of the passage opened; I saw the plates on the shelves, the lighted lamp on the long, oil-clothed table, 'Prepare to Meet Thy God' knitted over the fire-place, the smiling china dogs, the brown-stained settle, the grandmother clock, and I ran into the kitchen and into Annie's arms.

There was a welcome, then. The clock struck twelve as she kissed me, and I stood among the shining and striking like a prince taking off his disguise. One minute I was small and cold, skulking dead-scared down a black passage in my stiff, best suit, with my hollow belly thumping and my heart like a time bomb, clutching my grammar school cap, unfamiliar to myself, a snub-nosed story-teller lost in his own adventures and longing to be home; the next I was a royal nephew in smart town clothes, embraced and welcomed, standing in the snug centre of my stories and listening to the clock announcing me. She hurried me to the seat in the side of the cavernous fireplace and took off my shoes. The bright lamps and the ceremonial gongs blazed and rang for me.

She made a mustard bath and strong tea, told me to put on a pair of my cousin Gwilym's socks and an old coat of uncle's that smelt of rabbit and tobacco. She fussed and clucked and nodded and told me, as she cut bread and butter, how Gwilym was still studying to be a minister, and how Aunt Rach Morgan, who was ninety years old, had fallen on her belly on a scythe.

Then Uncle Jim came in like the devil with a red face and a wet nose and trembling, hairy hands. His walk was thick. He stumbled against the dresser and shook the coronation plates, and a lean cat shot booted out from the settle corner. Uncle looked nearly twice as tall as Annie. He could have carried her about under his coat and brought her out suddenly, a little, brown-skinned, toothless, hunchbacked woman with a cracked sing-song voice.

'You shouldn't have kept him out so long,' she said, angry and timid.

He sat down in his special chair, which was the broken throne of a bankrupt bard, and lit his pipe and stretched his legs and puffed clouds at the ceiling.

'He might catch his death of cold,' she said.

She talked at the back of his head while he wrapped himself in clouds. The cat slunk back. I sat at the table with my supper finished, and found a little empty bottle and a white balloon in the pockets of my coat.

'Run off to bed, there's a dear,' Annie whispered.

'Can I go and look at the pigs?'

'In the morning, dear,' she said.

So I said good night to Uncle Jim, who turned and smiled at me and winked through the smoke, and I kissed Annie and lit my candle.

'Good night.'

'Good night.'

'Good night.'

I climbed the stairs; each had a different voice. The house smelt of rotten wood and damp and animals. I thought that I had been walking long, damp passages all my life, and climbing stairs in the dark, alone. I stopped outside Gwilym's door on the draughty landing.

'Good night.'

The candle flame jumped in my bedroom where a lamp was burning very low, and the curtains waved; the water in a glass on a round table by the bed stirred, I thought, as the door closed, and lapped against the sides. There was a stream below the window; I thought it lapped against the house all night until I slept.

'Can I go and see the pigs?' I asked Gwilym next morning. The hollow fear of the house was gone, and, running downstairs to my breakfast, I smelt the sweetness of wood and the fresh spring grass and the quiet untidy farm-yard, with its tumbledown dirty-white cow-house and empty stables open.

Gwilym was a tall young man aged nearly twenty, with a thin stick of a body and spade-shaped face. You could dig the garden with him. He had a deep voice that cracked in half when he was excited, and he sang songs to himself, treble and bass, with the same sad hymn tune, and wrote hymns in the barn. He told me stories about girls who died for love. 'And she put a rope round the tree but it was too short,' he said; 'she stuck a pen-knife in her bosoms but it was too blunt.' We were sitting together on the straw heaps that day in the half-dark of the shuttered stable. He twisted and leaned near to me, raising his big finger, and the straw creaked.

'She jumped in the cold river, she jumped,' he said, his mouth against my ear, 'arse over tip and Diu, she was dead.' He squeaked like a bat.

The pigsties were at the far end of the yard. We walked towards them, Gwilym dressed in minister's black, though it was a weekday morning, and me in a serge suit with a darned bottom, past three hens scrabbling the muddy cobbles and a collie with one eye, sleeping with it open. The ramshackle outhouses had tumbling, rotten roofs, jagged holes in their sides, broken shutters, and peeling whitewash; rusty screws ripped out from the dangling, crooked boards; the lean cat of the night before sat snugly between the splintered jaws of bottles, cleaning its face, on the tip of the rubbish pile that rose triangular and smelling sweet and strong to the level of the riddled cart-house roof. There was nowhere like that farm-yard in all the slapdash county, nowhere so poor and grand and dirty as that square of mud and rubbish and bad wood and falling stone, where a bucketful of old and bedraggled hens scratched and laid small eggs. A duck quacked out of the trough in one deserted sty. Now a young man and a curly boy stood staring and sniffing over a wall at a sow, with its tits on the mud, giving suck.

'How many pigs are there?'

'Five. The bitch ate one,' said Gwilym.

We counted them as they squirmed and wriggled, rolled on their backs and bellies, edged and pinched and pushed and squealed about their mother. There were four. We counted again. Four pigs, four naked pink tails curling as up their mouths guzzled down and the sow grunted with pain and joy.

'She must have ate another,' I said, and picked up a scratching stick and prodded the grunting sow and rubbed her crusted bristles backwards. 'Or a fox jumped over the wall,' I said.

'It wasn't the sow or the fox,' said Gwilym. 'It was father.'

I could see uncle, tall and sly and red, holding the writhing pig in his two hairy hands, sinking his teeth in its thigh, crunching its trotters up: I could see him leaning over the wall of the sty with the pig's legs sticking out of his mouth. 'Did Uncle Jim eat the pig?'

Now, at this minute, behind the rotting sheds, he was standing, knee-deep in feathers, chewing off the live heads of the poultry.

'He sold it to go on the drink,' said Gwilym in his deepest rebuking whisper, his eyes fixed on the sky. 'Last

Christmas he took a sheep over his shoulder, and he was pissed for ten days.'

The sow rolled nearer the scratching stick, and the small pigs sucking at her, lost and squealing in the sudden darkness, struggling under her folds and pouches.

'Come and see my chapel,' said Gwilym. He forgot the lost pig at once and began to talk about the towns he had visited on a religious tour, Neath and Bridgend and Bristol and Newport, with their lakes and luxury gardens, their bright, coloured streets roaring with temptation. We walked away from the sty and the disappointed sow.

'I met actress after actress,' he said.

Gwilym's chapel was the last old barn before the field that led down to the river; it stood well above the farm-yard, on a mucky hill. There was one whole door with a heavy padlock, but you could get in easily through the holes on either side of it. He took out a ring of keys and shook them gently and tried each one in the lock. 'Very posh,' he said; 'I bought them from the junk-shop in Carmarthen.' We climbed into the chapel through a hole.

A dusty wagon with the name painted out and a white-wash cross on its side stood in the middle. 'My pulpit cart,' he said, and walked solemnly into it up the broken shaft. 'You sit on the hay; mind the mice,' he said. Then he brought out his deepest voice again, and cried to the heavens and the bat-lined rafters and the hanging webs: 'Bless us this holy day, O Lord, bless me and Dylan and this Thy little chapel for ever and ever, Amen. I've done a lot of improvements to this place.'

I sat on the hay and stared at Gwilym preaching, and heard his voice rise and crack and sink to a whisper and break into singing and Welsh and ring triumphantly and be wild and meek. The sun through a hole, shone on his praying shoulders, and he said: 'O God, Thou art everywhere all the time, in the dew of the morning, in the frost of the evening, in the field and the town, in the preacher and the sinner, in the sparrow and the big buzzard. Thou canst see everything, right down deep in our hearts; Thou canst see us when the sun is gone; Thou canst see us when there aren't any stars, in the gravy blackness, in the deep, deep, deep, deep pit; Thou canst see and spy and watch us all the time, in the little black corners, in the big cowboys' prairies, under the blankets when we're snoring fast, in the terrible shadows; pitch black, pitch black; Thou canst see everything we do, in the night and day, in the day and the night, everything, everything; Thou can't see all the time. O God, mun, you're like a bloody cat.'

He let his clasped hands fall. The chapel in the barn was still, and shafted with sunlight. There was nobody to cry Hallelujah or God-bless; I was too small and enamoured in the silence. The one duck quacked outside.

'Now I take a collection,' Gwilym said.

He stepped down from the cart and groped about in the hay beneath it and held out a battered tin to me.

'I haven't got a proper box,' he said.

I put two pennies in the tin,

'It's time for dinner,' he said, and we went back to the house without a word.

Annie said, when we had finished dinner: 'Put on your nice suit for this afternoon. The one with stripes.'

It was to be a special afternoon, for my best friend, Jack Williams, from Swansea, was coming down with his rich mother in a motor car, and Jack was to spend a fortnight's holiday with me.

'Where's Uncle Jim?'

'He's gone to market,' said Annie.

'Gwilym made a small pig's noise. We knew where uncle was; he was sitting in a public house with a heifer over his shoulder and two pigs nosing out of his pockets, and his lips wet with bull's blood.

'Is Mrs Williams very rich?' asked Gwilym.

I told him she had three motor cars and two houses,

which was a lie. 'She's the richest woman in Wales, and once she was a mayoress,' I said. 'Are we going to have tea in the best room?'

Annie nodded. 'And a large tin of peaches,' she said.

'That old tin's been in the cupboard since Christmas,' said Gwilym, 'mother's been keeping it for a day like this.'

'They're lovely peaches,' Annie said. She went upstairs to dress like Sunday.

The best room smelt of moth balls and fur and damp and dead plants and stale, sour air. Two glass cases on wooden coffin-boxes lined the window wall. You looked at the weed-grown vegetable garden through a stuffed fox's legs, over a partridge's head, along the red-paint-stained breast of a stiff wild duck. A case of china and pewter, trinkets, teeth, family brooches, stood beyond the bandy table; there was a large oil lamp on the patchwork table-cloth, a Bible with a clasp, a tall vase with a draped woman about to bathe on it, and a framed photograph of Annie, Uncle Jim, and Gwilym smiling in front of a fern-pot. On the mantelpiece were two clocks, some dogs, brass candle-sticks, a shepherdess, a man in a kilt, and a tinted photograph of Annie, with high hair and her breasts coming out. There were chairs around the table and in each corner, straight, curved, stained, padded, all with lace cloths hanging over their backs. A patched white sheet shrouded the harmonium. The fireplace was full of brass tongs, shovels, and pokers. The best room was rarely used. Annie dusted and brushed and polished there once a week, but the carpet still sent up a grey cloud when you trod on it, and dust lay evenly on the seats of the chairs, and balls of cotton and dirt and black stuffing and long black horse hairs were wedged in the cracks of the sofa. I blew on the glass to see the pictures. Gwilym and castles and cattle.

'Change your suit now,' said Gwilym.

I wanted to wear my old suit, to look like a proper farm boy and have manure in my shoes and hear it squelch as I walked, to see a cow have calves and a bull on top of a cow, to run down in the dingle and wet my stockings, to go out and shout, 'Come on, you b——,' and pelt the hens and talk in a proper voice. But I went upstairs to put my striped suit on.

From my bedroom I heard the noise of a motor car drawing up the yard. It was Jack Williams and his mother.

Gwilym shouted, 'They're here, in a Daimler!' from the foot of the stairs, and I ran down to meet them with my tie undone and my hair uncombed.

Annie was saying at the door: 'Good afternoon, Mrs Williams, good afternoon. Come right in, it's a lovely day, Mrs Williams. Did you have a nice journey then? This way, Mrs Williams, mind the step.'

Annie wore a black, shining dress that smelt of moth balls, like the chair covers in the best room; she had forgotten to change her gym-shoes, which were caked with mud and all holes. She fussed on before Mrs Williams down the stone passage, darting her head round, clucking, fidgeting, excusing the small house, anxiously tidying her hair with one rough, stubby hand.

Mrs Williams was tall and stout, with a jutting bosom and thick legs, her ankles swollen over her pointed shoes; she was fitted out like a mayoress or a ship, and she swayed after Annie into the best room.

She said: 'Please don't put yourself out for me, Mrs Jones, there's a dear.' She dusted the seat of a chair with a lace handkerchief from her bag before sitting down.

'I can't stop, you know,' she said.

'Oh, you must stay for a cup of tea,' said Annie, shifting and scraping the chairs away from the table so that nobody could move and Mrs Williams was hemmed in fast with her bosom and her rings and her bag, opening the china cupboard, upsetting the Bible on the floor, picking it up, dusting it hurriedly with her sleeve.

'And peaches,' Gwilym said. He was standing in the passage with his hat on.

Annie said, 'Take your hat off, Gwilym, make Mrs Williams comfortable,' and she put the lamp on the shrouded harmonium and spread out a white table-cloth that had a tea stain in the centre, and brought out the china and laid knives and cups for five.

'Don't bother about me, there's a dear,' said Mrs Williams. 'There's a lovely fox!' She flashed a finger of rings at the glass case.

'It's real blood,' I told Jack, and we climbed over the sofa to the table.

'No it isn't,' he said, 'it's red ink.'

'Oh, your shoes!' said Annie.

'Don't tread on the sofa, Jack, there's a dear.'

'If it isn't ink it's paint then.'

Gwilym said: 'Shall I get you a bit of cake, Mrs Williams?'

Annie rattled the tea-cups. 'There isn't a single bit of cake in the house,' she said; 'we forgot to order it from the shop; not a single bit. Oh, Mrs Williams!'

Mrs Williams said: 'Just a cup of tea thanks.' She was still sweating because she had walked all the way from the car. It spoiled her powder. She sparkled her rings and dabbed at her face.

'Three lumps,' she said. 'And I'm sure Jack will be very happy here.'

'Happy as sandboys.' Gwilym sat down.

'Now you must have some peaches, Mrs Williams, they're lovely.'

'They should be, they've been here long enough,' said Gwilym.

Annie rattled the tea-cups at him again.

'No peaches, thanks,' Mrs Williams said.

'Oh, you must, Mrs Williams, just one. With cream.'

'No, no, Mrs Jones, thanks the same,' she said. 'I don't mind pears or chunks, but I can't bear peaches.'

Jack and I had stopped talking. Anne stared down at her gymshoes. One of the clocks on the mantelpiece coughed, and struck. Mrs Williams struggled from her chair.

'There, time flies!' she said.

She pushed her way past the furniture, jostled against the sideboard, rattled the trinkets and brooches, and kissed Jack on the forehead.

'You've got scent on,' he said.

She patted my head.

'Now behave yourselves.'

To Annie, she said in a whisper: 'And remember, Mrs Jones, just good plain food. No spoiling his appetite.'

Annie followed her out of the room. She moved slowly now. 'I'll do my very best, Mrs Williams.'

We heard her say, 'Good-bye then, Mrs Williams,' and go down the steps of the kitchen and close the door. The motor car roared in the yard, then the noise grew softer and died.

Down the thick dingle Jack and I ran shouting, scalping the brambles with our thin stick-hatchets, dancing, hallooing. We skidded to a stop and prowled on the bushy banks of the stream. Up above, sat one-eyed, dead-eyed, sinister, slim, ten-notched Gwilym, loading his guns in Gallows Farm. We crawled and rattatted through the bushes, hid, at a whistled signal, in the deep grass, and crouched there, waiting for the crack of a twig or the secret breaking of boughs.

On my haunches, eager and alone, casting an ebony shadow, with the Gorsehill jungle swarming, the violent, impossible birds and fishes leaping, hidden under four-stemmed flowers the height of horses, in the early evening in a dingle near Carmarthen, my friend Jack Williams invisibly near me, I felt all my young body like an excited animal surrounding me, the torn knees bent, the bumping heart, the long heat and depth between the legs, the sweat prickling in the hands, the tunnels down to the eardrums, the little balls of dirt between the toes, the eyes in the sockets, the tucked-up voice, the blood racing, the memory around and within flying, jumping, swimming, and waiting to pounce. There, playing Indians in the evening, I was aware of me myself in the exact middle of a living story, and my body was my adventure and my name. I sprang with excitement and scrambled up through the scratching brambles again.

Jack cried: 'I see you! I see you!' He scampered after me. 'Bang! bang! you're dead!'

But I was young and loud and alive, though I lay down obediently.

'Now you try and kill me,' said Jack. 'Count a hundred.'

I closed one eye, saw him rush and stamp towards the upper field, then tiptoe back and begin to climb a tree, and I counted fifty and ran to the foot of the tree and killed him as he climbed. 'You fall down,' I said.

He refused to fall, so I climbed too, and we clung to the top branches and stared down at the lavatory in the corner of the field. Gwilym was sitting on the seat with his trousers down. He looked small and black. He was reading a book and moving his hands.

'We can see you!' we shouted.

He snatched his trousers up and put the book in his pocket.

'We can see you, Gwilym!'

He came out into the field. 'Where are you, then?'

We waved our caps at him.

'In the sky!' Jack shouted.

'Flying!' I shouted.

We stretched our arms out like wings.

'Fly down here.'

We swung and laughed on the branches.

'There's birds!' cried Gwilym.

Our jackets were torn and our stockings were wet and our shoes were sticky; we had green moss and brown bark on our hands and faces when we went in for supper and a scolding. Annie was quiet that night, though she called me a ragamuffin and said she didn't know what Mrs Williams would think and told Gwilym he should know better. We made faces at Gwilym and put salt in his tea, but after supper he said: 'You can come to the chapel if you like. Just before bed.'

He lit a candle on the top of the pulpit cart. It was a small light in the big barn. The bats were gone. Shadows still clung upside down along the roof. Gwilym was no longer my cousin in a Sunday suit, but a tall stranger shaped like a spade in a cloak, and his voice grew too deep. The straw heaps were lively. I thought of the sermon on the cart: we were watched, Jack's heart was watched, Gwilym's tongue was marked down, my whisper, 'Look at the little eyes,' was remembered always.

'Now I take confessions,' said Gwilym from the cart.

Jack and I stood bareheaded in the circle of the candle, and I could feel the trembling of Jack's body.

'You first.' Gwilym's finger, as bright as though he had held it in the candle flame until it burned, pointed me out, and I took a step towards the pulpit cart, raising my head.

'Now you confess,' said Gwilym.

'What have I got to confess?'

'The worst thing you've done.'

I let Edgar Reynolds be whipped because I had taken his homework; I stole from my mother's bag; I stole from Gwyneth's bag; I stole twelve books in three visits from the library, and threw them away in the park; I drank a cup of my water to see what it tasted like; I beat a dog with a stick so that it would roll over and lick my hand afterwards; I looked with Dan Jones through the keyhole while his maid had a bath; I cut my knee with a penknife, and put the blood on my handkerchief and said it had come out of my ears so that I could pretend I was ill and frighten my mother; I pulled my trousers down and showed Jack Williams; I saw Billy Jones beat a pigeon to death with a fire-shovel, and laughed and got sick; Cedric Williams and I broke into Mrs Samuels' house and poured ink over the bedclothes.

I said: 'I haven't done anything bad.'

'Go on, confess,' said Gwilym. He was frowning down at me.

'I can't! I can't!' I said. 'I haven't done anything bad.'

'Go on, confess!'

'I won't! I won't!'

Jack began to cry. 'I want to go home,' he said.

Gwilym opened the chapel door and we followed him into the yard, down past the black, humped sheds, towards the house, and Jack sobbed all the way.

In bed together, Jack and I confessed our sins.

'I steal from my mother's bag, too; there are pounds and pounds.'

'How much do you steal?'

'Threepence.'

'I killed a man once.'

'No you didn't then.'

'Honest to Christ, I shot him through the heart.'

'What was his name?'

'Williams.'

'Did he bleed?'

I thought the stream was lapping against the house.

'Like a bloody pig,' I said.

Jack's tears had dried. 'I don't like Gwilym, he's barmy.'

'No he isn't. I found a lot of poems in his bedroom once. They were all written to girls. And he showed them to me afterwards, and he'd changed all the girls' names to God.'

'He's religious.'

'No he isn't, he goes with actresses. He knows Corinne Griffith.'

Our door was open. I liked the door locked at night, because I would rather have a ghost in the bedroom than think of one coming in; but Jack liked it open, and we tossed and he won. We heard the front door rattle and footsteps in the kitchen passage.

'That's Uncle Jim.'

72

'What's he like?'

'He's like a fox, he eats pigs and chickens.'

The ceiling was thin and we heard every sound, the creaking of the bard's chair, the clatter of plates, Annie's voice saying: 'Midnight!'

'He's drunk,' I said. We lay quite still, hoping to hear a quarrel.

'Perhaps he'll throw plates,' I said.

But Annie scolded him softly. 'There's a fine state, Jim.'

He murmured to her.

'There's one pig gone,' she said. 'Oh, why do you have to do it, Jim? There's nothing left now. We'll never be able to carry on.'

'Money! money! money!' he said. I knew he would be lighting his pipe.

Then Annie's voice grew so soft we could not hear the words, and uncle said: 'Did she pay you the thirty shillings?'

'They're talking about your mother,' I told Jack.

For a long time Annie spoke in a low voice, and we waited for words. 'Mrs Williams,' she said, and 'motor car', and 'Jack,' and 'peaches.' I thought she was crying for her voice broke on the last word.

Uncle Jim's chair creaked again, he might have struck his fist on the table, and we heard him shout: 'I'll give her peaches! Peaches, peaches! Who does she think she is? Aren't peaches good enough for her? To hell with her bloody motor car and her bloody son! Making us small.'

'Don't, don't Jim!' Annie said, 'you'll wake the boys.'

'I'll wake them and whip the hell out of them, too!'

'Please, please, Jim!'

'You send the boy away,' he said, 'or I'll do it myself. Back to his three bloody houses.'

Jack pulled the bedclothes over his head and sobbed into the pillow: 'I don't want to hear, I don't want to hear. I'll write to my mother. She'll take me away.'

I climbed out to close the door. Jack would not talk to

me again, and I fell asleep to the noise of the voices below, which soon grew gentle.

Uncle Jim was not at breakfast. When we came down, Jack's shoes were cleaned for him and his jacket was darned and pressed. Annie gave two boiled eggs to Jack and one to me. She forgave me when I drank tea from the saucer.

After breakfast, Jack walked to the post office. I took the one-eyed collie to chase rabbits in the upper fields, but it barked at ducks and brought me a tramp's shoe from a hedge, and lay down with its tail wagging in a rabbit hole. I threw stones at the deserted duck pond, and the collie ambled back with sticks.

Jack went skulking into the damp dingle, his hands in his pockets, his cap over one eye. I left the collie sniffing at a molehill, and climbed to the tree-top in the corner of the lavatory field. Below me, Jack was playing Indians all alone, scalping through the bushes, surprising himself round a tree, hiding from himself in the grass. I called to him once, but he pretended not to hear. He played alone, silently and savagely. I saw him standing with his hands in his pockets, swaying like a Kelly, on the mudbank by the stream at the foot of the dingle. My bough lurched, the heads of the dingle bushes spun up towards me like green tops. 'I'm falling!' I cried, my trousers saved me, I swung and grasped, this was one minute of wild adventure, but Jack did not look up and the minute was lost. I climbed, without dignity, to the ground.

Early in the afternoon, after a silent meal, when Gwilym was reading the scriptures or writing hymns to girls or sleeping in his chapel, Annie was baking bread, and I was cutting a wooden whistle in the loft over the stable, the motor car drove up in the yard again.

Out of the house Jack, in his best suit, ran to meet his mother, and I heard him say as she stepped, raising her short skirts, on to the cobbles: 'And he called you a bloody cow, and he said he'd whip the hell out of me, and Gwilym took me to the barn in the dark and let the mice run over me, and Dylan's a thief, and that old woman's spoilt my jacket.'

Mrs Williams sent the chauffeur for Jack's luggage. Annie came to the door, trying to smile and curtsy, tidying her hair, wiping her hands on her pinafore.

Mrs Williams said, 'Good afternoon,' and sat with Jack in the back of the car and stared at the ruin of Gorsehill.

The chauffeur came back. The car drove off, scattering the hens. I ran out of the stable to wave to Jack. He sat still and stiff by his mother's side. I waved my handkerchief.

OLD GARBO

Mr Farr trod delicately and disgustedly down the dark, narrow stairs like a man on ice. He knew, without looking or slipping, that vicious boys had littered the darkest corners with banana peel; and when he reached the lavatory, the basins would be choked and the chains snapped on purpose. He remembered 'Mr Farr, no father' scrawled in brown, and the day the sink was full of blood that nobody admitted having lost. A girl rushed past him up the stairs, knocked the papers out of his hand, did not apologize, and the loose meg of his cigarette burned his lower lip as he failed to open the lavatory door. I heard from inside his protest and rattlings, the sing-song whine of his voice, the stamping of his small patent-leather shoes, his favourite swear-words – he swore, violently and privately, like a collier used to thinking in the dark – and I let him in.

'Do you always lock the door?' he asked, scurrying to the tiled wall.

'It stuck,' I said.

He shivered, and buttoned.

He was the senior reporter, a great shorthand writer, a chain-smoker, a bitter drinker, very humorous, round-faced and round-bellied, with dart holes in his nose. Once, I thought as I stared at him then in the lavatory of the offices of the *Tawe News*, he might have been a mincing-mannered man, with a strut and a cane to balance it, a watch-chain across the waistcoat, a gold tooth, even, perhaps a flower from his own garden in his buttonhole. But now each attempt at a precise gesture was caked and soaked before it began; when he placed the tips of his thumb and forefinger together, you saw only the cracked nails in mourning and the Woodbine stains. He gave me a cigarette and shook his coat to hear matches.

'Here's a light, Mr Farr,' I said.

It was good to keep in with him; he covered all the big stories, the occasional murder, such as when Thomas O'Connor used a bottle on his wife – but that was before my time – the strikes, the best fires. I wore my cigarette as he did, a hanging badge of bad habits.

'Look at that word on the wall,' he said. 'Now that's ugly. There's a time and a place.'

Winking at me, scratching his bald patch as though the thought came from there, he said: 'Mr Solomon wrote that.'

Mr Solomon was the news editor and a Wesleyan.

'Old Solomon,' said Mr Farr, 'he'd cut every baby in half just for pleasure.'

I smiled and said: 'I bet he would!' But I wished that I could have answered in such a way as to show for Mr Solomon the disrespect I did not feel. This was a great male moment, and the most enjoyable since I had begun work three weeks before: leaning against the cracked tiled wall, smoking and smiling, looking down at my shoe scraping circles on the wet floor, sharing a small wickedness with an old, important man. I should have been writing up last night's performance of *The Crucifixion* or loitering, with my new hat on one side, through the Christmas-Saturday-crowded town in the hopes of an accident.

'You must come along with me one night,' Mr Farr said slowly. 'We'll go down the "Fishguard" on the docks; you can see the sailors knitting there in the public bar. Why not tonight? And there's shilling women in the "Lord Jersey". You stick to Woodbines, like me.'

He washed his hands as a young boy does, wiping the dirt on the roll-towel, stared in the mirror over the basin, twirled the ends of his moustache, and saw them droop again immediately after.

'Get to work,' he said.

I walked into the lobby, leaving him with his face pressed to the glass and one finger exploring his bushy nostrils.

It was nearly eleven o'clock, and time for a cocoa or a

Russian tea in the Café Royal, above the tobacconist's in High Street, where junior clerks and shop assistants and young men working in their fathers' offices or articled to stock brokers and solicitors meet every morning for gossip and stories. I made my way through the crowds: the Valley men, up for the football; the country shoppers, the window gazers; the silent, shabby men at the corners of the packed streets, standing in isolation in the rain; the press of mothers and prams; old women in black, brooched dresses carrying frails, smart girls with shining mackintoshes and splashed stockings; little, dandy lascars, bewildered by the weather; business men with wet spats; through a mushroom forest of umbrellas; and all the time I thought of the paragraphs I would never write. I'll put you all in a story by and by.

Mrs Constable, laden and red with shopping, recognized me as she charged out of Woolworth's like a bull. 'I haven't seen your mother for ages! Oh! this Christmas rush! Remember me to Florrie. I'm going to have a cup of tea at the "Modern". There,' she said, 'I've lost a pan!'

I saw Percy Lewis, who put chewing gum in my hair at school.

A tall man stared at the doorway of a hat shop, resisting the crowds, standing hard and still. All the moving irrelevancies of good news grew and acted around me as I reached the café entrance and climbed the stairs.

'What's for you, Mr Swaffer?'

'The usual, please.' Cocoa and free biscuit.

Most of the boys were there already. Some wore the outlines of moustaches, others had sideboards and crimped hair, some smoked curved pipes and talked with them gripped between their teeth, there were pin-stripe trousers and hard collars, one daring bowler.

'Sit by here,' said Leslie Bird. He was in the boots at Dan Lewis's.

'Been to the flicks this week, Thomas?'

'Yes. The Regal. *White Lies*. Damned good show, too!

Connie Bennett was great! Remember her in the foam-bath, Leslie?'

'Too much foam for me, old man.'

The broad vowels of the town were narrowed in, the rise and fall of the family accent was caught and pressed.

At the top window of the International Stores across the street a group of uniformed girls were standing with tea-cups in their hands. One of them waved a handkerchief. I wondered if she waved it to me. 'There's that dark piece again,' I said. 'She's got her eye on you.'

'They look all right in their working clothes,' he said. 'You catch them when they're all dolled up, they're awful. I knew a little nurse once, she looked a peach in her uniform, really refined; no, really, I mean. I picked her up on the prom one night. She was in her Sunday best. There's a difference; she looked like a bit of Marks and Spencer's.' As he talked he was looking through the window with the corners of his eyes.

The girl waved again, and turned away to giggle.

'Pretty cheap!' he said.

I said: 'And little Audrey laughed and laughed.'

He took out a plated cigarette case. 'Present,' he said. 'I bet my uncle with three balls has it in a week. Have a best Turkish.'

His matches were marked Allsopps. 'Got them from the "Carlton"' he said. 'Pretty girl behind the bar: knows her onions. You've never been there, have you? Why don't you drop in for one to-night? Gil Morris'll be there, too. We usually sink a couple Saturdays. There's a hop at the "Melba".'

'Sorry,' I said. 'I'm going out with our senior reporter. Some other time, Leslie. So long!'

I paid my threepence.

'Good morning, Cassie.'

'Good morning, Hannen.'

The rain had stopped and High Street shone. Walking on the tram-lines, a neat man held his banner high and

prominently feared the Lord. I knew him as a Mr Mat-
thews, who had been saved some years ago from British
port and who now walked every night, in rubber shoes
with a prayer book and a flashlight, through the lanes.
There went Mr Evans the Produce through the side-door
of the 'Bugle'. Three typists rushed by for lunch, poached
egg and milk-shake, leaving a lavender scent. Should I take
the long way through the Arcade, and stop to look at the
old man with the broken, empty pram who always stood
there, by the music store, and who would take off his cap
and set his hair alight for a penny? It was only a trick to
amuse boys, and I took the short cut down Chapel Street,
on the edge of the slum called the Strand, past the enticing
Italian chip shop where young men who had noticing
parents bought twopennyworth on late nights to hide their
breath before the last tram home. Then up the narrow
office stairs and into the reporters' room.

Mr Solomon was shouting down the telephone. I heard
the last words: 'You're just a dreamer, Williams.' He put
the receiver down. 'That boy's a buddy dreamer,' he said to
no one. He never swore.

I finished my report of *The Crucifixion* and handed it to
Mr Farr.

'Too much platitudinous verbosity.'

Half an hour later, Ted Williams, dressed to golf, sidled
in, smiling, thumbed his nose at Mr Solomon's back, and
sat quietly in a corner with a nail-file.

I whispered: 'What was he slanging you for?'

'I went out on a suicide, a tram conductor called Hop-
kins, and the widow made me stay and have a cup of tea.
That's all.' He was very winning in his ways, more like a
girl than a man who dreamed of Fleet Street and spent his
summer fortnight walking up and down past the *Daily
Express* office and looking for celebrities in the pubs.

Saturday was my free afternoon. It was one o'clock and
time to leave, but I stayed on; Mr Farr said nothing. I pretended to be busy scribbling words and caricaturing with

no likeness Mr Solomon's toucan profile and the snub copy-boy who whistled out of tune behind the windows of the telephone box. I wrote my name, 'Reporters' Room, *Tawe News*, Tawe, South Wales, England, Europe, The Earth'. And a list of books I had not written: 'Land of My Fathers, a Study of the Welsh Character in all its Aspects'; 'Eighteen, a Provincial Autobiography'; 'The Merciless Ladies, a Novel'. Still Mr Farr did not look up. I wrote 'Hamlet'. Surely Mr Farr, stubbornly transcribing his council notes had not forgotten. I heard Mr Solomon mutter, leaning over his shoulder: 'To aitch with Alderman Daniels.' Half-past one. Ted was in a dream. I spent a long time putting on my overcoat, tied my Old Grammarian's scarf one way and then another.

'Some people are too lazy to take their half-days off,' said Mr Farr suddenly. 'Six o'clock in the "Lamps" back bar.' He did not turn round or stop writing.

'Going for a nice walk?' asked my mother.

'Yes, on the common. Don't keep tea waiting.'

I went to the Plaza. 'Press,' I said to the girl with the Tyrolean hat and skirt.

'There's been two reporters this week.'

'Special notice.'

She showed me to a seat. During the educational film, with the rude seeds hugging and sprouting in front of my eyes and plants like arms and legs, I thought of the bob women and the pansy sailors in the dives. There might be a quarrel with razors, and once Ted Williams found a lip outside the Mission to Seamen. It had a small moustache. The sinuous plants danced on the screen. If only Tawe were a larger sea-town, there would be curtained rooms underground with blue films. The potato's life came to an end. Then I entered an American college and danced with the president's daughter. The hero, called Lincoln, tall and dark with good teeth, I displaced quickly, and the girl spoke my name as she held his shadow, the singing college chorus in sailors' hats and bathing dresses called me big boy and king, Jack Oakie and I sped up the field, and on the shoulders of the crowd the president's daughter and I brought across the shifting-coloured curtain with a kiss that left me giddy and bright-eyed as I walked out of the cinema into the strong lamplight and the new rain.

A whole wet hour to waste in the crowds. I watched the queue outside the Empire and studied the posters of *Nuit de Paris*, and thought of the long legs and startling faces of the chorus girls I had seen walking arm in arm, earlier that week, up and down the streets in the winter sunshine, their mouths, I remembered remarking and treasuring for the first page of 'The Merciless Ladies' that was never begun, like crimson scars, their hair raven-black or silver; their scent and paint reminded me of the hot and chocolate-coloured East, their eyes were pools. Lola de Kenway, Babs Courcey, Ramona Day would be with me all my life. Until I died, of a wasting, painless disease, and spoke my prepared last words, they would always walk with me, recalling me to my dead youth in the vanished High Street nights when the shop windows were blazing, and singing out of the pubs, and sirens from the Haford sat in the steaming chip shops with their handbags on their knees and their ear-rings rattling. I stopped to look at the window of Dirty Black's, the Fancy Man, but it was innocent; there were only itching and sneezing powders, stink bombs, rubber pens, and Charlie masks; all the novelties were inside, but I dared not go in for fear a woman would serve me, Mrs Dirty Black with a moustache and knowing eyes, or a thin, dog-faced girl I saw there once, who winked and smelt of seaweed. In the market I bought pink cachous. You never knew.

The back room of 'The Three Lamps' was full of elderly men. Mr Farr had not arrived. I leant against the bar, between an alderman and a solicitor, drinking bitter, wishing that my father could see me now and glad, at the same time, that he was visiting Uncle A in Aberavon. He could not fail to see that I was a boy no longer, nor fail to be angry at the angle of my fag and my hat and the threat of the clutched tankard. I liked the taste of beer, its live, white lather, its brass-bright depths, the sudden world through the wet brown walls of the glass, the tilted rush to the lips and the slow swallowing down to the lapping belly, the salt on the tongue, the foam at the corners.

'Same again, miss.' She was middle-aged. 'One for you, miss?'

'Not during hours, ta all the same.'

'You're welcome.'

Was that an invitation to drink with her afterwards, to wait at the back door until she glided out, and then to walk through the night, along the promenade and sands, on to a soft dune where couples lay loving under their coats and looking at the Mumbles lighthouse? She was plump and plain, her netted hair was auburn and wisped with grey. She gave me my change like a mother giving her boy pennies for the pictures, and I would not go out with her if she put cream on it.

Mr Farr hurried down High Street, savagely refusing laces and matches, averting his eyes from the shabby crowds. He knew that the poor and the sick and the ugly, unwanted people were so close around him that, with one look of recognition, one gesture of sympathy, he would be lost among them and the evening would be spoiled for ever.

'You're a pint man then,' he said at my elbow.

'Good evening, Mr Farr. Only now and then for a change. 'What's yours? Dirty night,' I said.

Safe in a prosperous house, out of the way of the rain and the unsettling streets, where the poor and the past could not touch him, he took his glass lazily in the company of business and professional men and raised it to the light. 'It's going to get dirtier,' he said. 'You wait till the "Fishguard". Here's health! You can see the sailors knitting there. And the old fish-girls in the "Jersey". Got to go to the w. for a breath of fresh air.'

Mr Evans the Produce came in quickly through a side door hidden by curtains, whispered his drink, shielded it with his overcoat, swallowed it in secrecy.

'Similar,' said Mr Farr, 'and half for his nibs.'

The bar was too high class to look like Christmas. A notice said 'No Ladies'.

We left Mr Evans gulping in his tent.

Children screamed in Goat Street, and one boy, out of season, pulled my sleeve, crying: 'Penny for the guy!' Big women in men's caps barricaded their doorways, and a posh girl gave us the wink at the corner of the green iron convenience opposite the Carlton Hotel. We entered to music, the bar was hung with ribbons and balloons, a tubercular tenor clung to the piano, behind the counter Leslie Bird's pretty barmaid was twitting a group of young men who leant far over and asked to see her garters and invited her to gins and limes and lonely midnight walks and moist adventures in the cinema. Mr Farr sneered down his glass as I watched the young men enviously and saw how much she liked their ways, how she slapped their hands lightly and wriggled back, in pride of her prettiness and gaiety, to pull the beer-handles.

'Toop little Twms from the Valleys. There'll be some puking to-night,' he said with pleasure.

Other young men, sleek-haired, pale, and stocky, with high cheek-bones and deep eyes, bright ties, double-breasted waistcoats and wide trousers, some pocked from the pits, their broad hands scarred and damaged, all exultantly half-drunk, stood singing round the piano, and the tenor with the fallen chest led in a clear voice. Oh! to be able to join in the suggestive play or the rocking choir, to shout *Bread of Heaven*, with my shoulders back and my arms linked with Little Moscow, or to be called 'saucy' and 'a one' as I joked and ogled at the counter, making innocent, dirty love that could come to nothing among the spilt beer and piling glasses.

'Let's get away from the bloody nightingales,' said Mr Farr.

'Too much bloody row,' I said.

'Now we're coming to somewhere.' We crawled down Strand alleys by the side of the mortuary, through a gas-lit lane where hidden babies cried together and reached the 'Fishguard' door as a man, muffled like Mr Evans, slid out in front of us with a bottle or a black-jack in one gloved hand. The bar was empty. An old man whose hands trembled sat behind the counter, staring at his turnip watch.

'Merry Christmas, Pa.'

'Good evening, Mr F.'

'Drop of rum, Pa.'

A red bottle shook over two glasses.

'Very special poison, son.'

'This'll make your eyes bulge,' said Mr Farr.

My iron head stood high and firm, no sailors' rum could rot the rock of my belly. Poor Leslie Bird the port-sipper, and little Gil Morris who marked dissipation under his eyes with a blacklead every Saturday night, I wished they could have seen me now, in the dark, stunted room with photographs of boxers peeling on the wall.

'More poison, Pa,' I said.

'Where's the company tonight? gone to the Riviera?'

'They're in the snuggery, Mr F, there's a party for Mrs Prothero's daughter.'

In the back room, under a damp royal family, a row of black-dressed women on a hard bench sat laughing and crying, short glasses lined by their Guinnesses. On an opposite bench two men in jerseys drank appreciatively, nodding at the emotions of the women. And on the one chair, in the middle of the room, an old woman, with a bonnet tied under her chins, a feather boa, and white gym-shoes, tittered and wept above the rest. We sat on the men's bench. One of the two touched his cap with a sore hand.

'What's the party, Jack?' asked Mr Farr. 'Meet my colleague, Mr Thomas; this is Jack Stiff, the mortuary keeper.'

Jack Stiff spoke from the side of his mouth. 'It's Mrs Prothero there. We call her Old Garbo because she isn't like her, see. She had a message from the hospital about an hour ago, Mrs Harris's Winifred brought it here, to say her second daughter's died in pod.'

'Baby girl dead, too,' said the man at his side.

'So all the old girls came round to sympathize, and they made a big collection for her, and now she's beginning to drink it up and treating round. We've had a couple of pints from her already.'

'Shameful!'

The rum burned and kicked in the hot room, but my head felt tough as a hill and I could write twelve books before morning and roll the 'Carlton' barmaid, like a barrel, the length of Tawe sands.

'Drinks for the troops!'

Before a new audience, the women cried louder, patting Mrs Prothero's knees and hands, adjusting her bonnet, praising her dead daughter.

'What'll you have, Mrs Prothero, dear?'

'No, have it with me, dear, best in the house.'

'Well, a Guinness tickles my fancy.'

'And a little something in it, dear.'

'Just for Margie's sake, then.'

'Think if she was here now, dear, singing *One of the Ruins* or *Cockles and Mussels*; she had a proper madam's voice.'

'Oh, don't, Mrs Harris!'

'There, we're only bucking you up. Grief killed the cat, Mrs Prothero. Let's have a song together, dear.'

'The pale moon was rising above the grey mountain,
The sun was declining beneath the blue sea,
When I strolled with my love to the pure crystal fountain.

Mrs Prothero sang.

'It was her daughter's favourite song,' said Jack Stiff's friend.

Mr Farr tapped me on the shoulder; his hand fell slowly from a great height and his thin, bird's voice spoke from a whirring circle on the ceiling. 'A drop of out-of-doors for you and me.' The gamps and bonnets, the white gym-shoes, the bottles and the mildew king, the singing mortuary man, the *Rose of Tralee*, swam together in the snuggery; two small men, Mr Farr and his twin brother, led me on an ice-rink to the door, and the night air slapped me down. The evening happened suddenly. A wall slumped over and knocked off my trilby; Mr Farr's brother disappeared under the cobbles. Here came a wall like a buffalo; dodge him, son. Have a drop of angostura, have a drop of brandy, Fernet Branca, Polly, Ooo! the mother's darling! have a hair of the dog.

'Feeling better now?'

I sat in a plush chair I had never seen before, sipping a mothball drink and appreciating an argument between Ted Williams and Mr Farr. Mr Farr was saying sternly: 'You came in here to look for sailors.'

'No, I didn't then,' said Ted. 'I came for local colour.'

The notices on the walls were: ' "The Lord Jersey". Prop.: Titch Thomas.' 'No Betting.' 'No Swearing, B—— you.' 'The Lord helps Himself, but you mustn't.' 'No Ladies allowed, except Ladies.'

'This is a funny pub,' I said. 'See the notices?'

'Okay now?'

'I'm feeling upsydaisy.'

'There's a pretty girl for you. Look, she's giving you the glad.'

'But she's got no nose.'

My drink, like winking, had turned itself into beer. A hammer tapped. 'Order! order!' At a sound in a new saloon a collarless chairman with a cigar called on Mr Jenkins to provide *The Lily of Laguna*.

'By request,' said Mr Jenkins.

'Order! order! for Katie Sebastopol Street. What is it, Katie?'

She sang the National Anthem.

'Mr Fred Jones will supply his usual dirty one.'

A broken baritone voice spoiled the chorus: I recognized it as my own, and drowned it.

A girl of the Salvation Army avoided the arms of two firemen and sold them a *War Cry*.

A young man with a dazzling handkerchief round his head, black and white holiday shoes with holes for the toes, and no socks, danced until the bar cried: 'Mabel!'

Ted clapped at my side. 'That's style! "Nijinsky of the Nightworld," there's a story! Wonder if I can get an interview?'

'Half a crack,' said Mr Farr.

'Don't make me cross.'

A wind from the docks tore up the street, I heard the rowdy dredger in the bay and a boat blowing to come in, the gas-lamps bowed and bent, then again smoke closed about the stained walls with George and Mary dripping above the women's bench, and Jack Stiff whispered, holding his hand in front of him like the paw of an animal: 'Old Garbo's gone.'

The sad and jolly women huddled together.

'Mrs Harris's little girl got the message wrong. Old Garbo's daughter's right as rain, the baby was born dead. Now the old girls want their money back, but they can't find Garbo anywhere.' He licked his hand. 'I know where she's gone.'

His friend said: 'To a boozer over the bridge.'

In low voices the women reviled Mrs Prothero, liar, adulteress, mother of bastards, thief.

'She got you know what.'

'Never cured it.'

'Got Charlie tattooed on her.'

'Three and eight she owes me.'

'Two and ten.'

'Money for my teeth.'

'One and a tanner out of my Old Age.'

Who kept filling my glass? Beer ran down my cheek and my collar. My mouth was full of saliva. The bench spun. The cabin of the 'Fishguard' tilted. Mr Farr retreated slowly; the telescope twisted, and his face, with wide and hairy nostrils, breathed against mine.

'Mr Thomas is going to get sick.'

'Mind your brolly, Mrs Arthur.'

'Take his head.'

The last tram clanked home. I did not have the penny for the fare. 'You get off here. Careful!' The revolving hill to my father's house reached to the sky. Nobody was up. I crept to a wild bed, and the wallpaper lakes converged and sucked me down.

Sunday was a quiet day, though St Mary's bells, a mile away, rang on, long after church time, in the holes of my head. Knowing that I would never drink again, I lay in bed until midday dinner and remembered the unsteady shapes and far-off voices of the ten o'clock town. I read the newspapers. All news was bad that morning, but an article called 'Our Lord was a Flower-lover' moved me to tears of bewilderment and contrition. I excused myself from the Sunday joint and three vegetables.

In the park in the afternoon I sat alone near the deserted bandstand. I caught a ball of waste paper that the wind blew down the gravel path towards the rockery, and, straightening it out and holding it on my knee, wrote the first three lines of a poem without hope. A dog nosed me out where I crouched, behind a bare tree in the cold, and rubbed its nose against my hand. 'My only friend,' I said. It stayed with me up to the early dusk, sniffing and scratching.

On Monday morning, with shame and hate, afraid to look at them again, I destroyed the article and the poem, throwing the pieces on to the top of the wardrobe, and I told Leslie Bird in the tram to the office: 'You should have been with us, Saturday, Christ!'

Early on Tuesday night, which was Christmas Eve, I walked, with a borrowed half-crown, into the back room of the 'Fishguard'. Jack Stiff was alone. The women's bench was covered with sheets of newspaper. A bunch of balloons hung from the lamp.

'Here's health!'

'Merry Christmas!'

'Where's Mrs Prothero?'

His hand was bandaged now. 'Oh! You haven't heard? She spent all the collection money. She took it over the bridge to the "Heart's Delight". She didn't let one of the old girls see her. It was over a pound. She'd spent a lot of it before they found her daughter wasn't dead. She couldn't face them then. Have this one with me. So she finished it up by stop-tap Monday. Then a couple of men from the banana boats saw her walking across the bridge, and she stopped half-way. But they weren't in time'.

'Merry Christmas!'

'We got a pair of gym-shoes on our slab.'

None of Old Garbo's friends came in that night.

When I showed this story a long time later to Mr Farr, he said: 'You got it all wrong. You got the people mixed. The boy with the handkerchief danced in the "Jersey". Fred Jones was singing in the "Fishguard". Never mind. Come and have one to-night in the "Nelson". There's a girl down there who'll show you where the sailor bit her. And there's a policeman who knew Jack Johnson.'

'I'll put them all in a story by and by,' I said.

AFTER THE FAIR

The fair was over, the lights in the coconut stalls were put out, and the wooden horses stood still in the darkness, waiting for the music and the hum of the machines that would set them trotting forward. One by one, in every booth, the naphtha jets were turned down and the canvases pulled over the little gaming tables. The crowd went home, and there were lights in the windows of the caravans.

Nobody had noticed the girl. In her black clothes she stood against the side of the roundabouts, hearing the last feet tread upon the sawdust and the last voices die in the distance. Then, all alone on the deserted ground, surrounded by the shapes of wooden horses and cheap fairy boats, she looked for a place to sleep. Now here and now there, she raised the canvas that shrouded the coconut stalls and peered into the warm darkness. She was frightened to step inside, and as a mouse scampered across the littered shavings on the floor, or as the canvas creaked and a rush of wind set it dancing, she ran away and hid again near the roundabouts. Once she stepped on the boards; the bells round a horse's throat jingled and were still; she did not dare breathe again until all was quiet and the darkness had forgotten the noise of the bells. Then here and there she went peeping for a bed, into each gondola, under each tent. But there was nowhere, nowhere in all the fair for her to sleep. One place was too silent, and in another was the noise of mice. There was straw in the corner of the Astrologer's tent, but it moved as she touched it; she knelt by its side and put out her hand; she felt a baby's hand upon her own.

Now there was nowhere, so slowly she turned towards the caravans on the outskirts of the field, and found all but two to be unlit. She waited, clutching her empty bag, and wondering which caravan she should disturb. At last she decided to knock upon the window of the little, shabby one near her, and, standing on tiptoes, she looked in. The fattest man she had ever seen was sitting in front of the stove, toasting a piece of bread. She tapped three times on the glass, then hid in the shadows. She heard him come to the top of the steps and call out 'Who? Who?' but she dare not answer. 'Who? Who?' he called again.

She laughed at his voice which was as thin as he was fat.

He heard her laughter and turned to where the darkness concealed her. 'First you tap,' he said, 'then you hide, then you laugh.'

She stepped into the circle of light, knowing she need no longer hide herself.

'A girl,' he said. 'Come in, and wipe your feet.' He did not wait but retreated into his caravan, and she could do nothing but follow him up the steps and into the crowded room. He was seated again, and toasting the same piece of bread. 'Have you come in?' he said, for his back was towards her.

'Shall I close the door?' she asked, and closed it before he replied.

She sat on the bed and watched him toast the bread until it burnt.

'I can toast better than you,' she said.

'I don't doubt it,' said the Fat Man.

She watched him put the charred toast upon a plate by his side, take another round of bread and hold that, too, in front of the stove. It burnt very quickly.

'Let me toast it for you,' she said. Ungraciously he handed her the fork and the loaf.

'Cut it,' he said, 'toast it, and eat it.'

She sat on the chair.

'See the dent you've made on my bed,' said the Fat Man. 'Who are you to come in and dent my bed?'

'My name is Annie,' she told him.

Soon all the bread was toasted and buttered, so she put it in the centre of the table and arranged two chairs.

'I'll have mine on the bed,' said the Fat Man. 'You'll have it here.'

When they had finished their supper, he pushed back his chair and stared at her across the table.

'I am the Fat Man,' he said. 'My home is Treorchy; the Fortune-Teller next door is Aberdare.'

'I am nothing to do with the fair,' she said, 'I am Cardiff.'

'There's a town,' agreed the Fat Man. He asked her why she had come away.

'Money,' said Annie.

Then he told her about the fair and the places he had been to and the people he had met. He told her his age and his weight and the names of his brothers and what he would call his son. He showed her a picture of Boston Harbour and the photograph of his mother who lifted weights. He told her how summer looked in Ireland.

'I've always been a fat man,' he said, 'and now I'm the Fat Man; there's nobody to touch me for fatness.' He told her of a heat-wave in Sicily and of the Mediterranean Sea. She told him of the baby in the Astrologer's tent.

'That's the stars again,' he said.

'The baby'll die,' said Annie.

He opened the door and walked out into the darkness. She looked about her but did not move, wondering if he had gone to fetch a policeman. It would never do to be caught by the policeman again. She stared through the open door into the inhospitable night and drew her chair closer to the stove.

'Better to be caught in the warmth,' she said. But she trembled at the sound of the Fat Man approaching, and pressed her hands upon her thin breast as he climbed up the steps like a walking mountain. She could see him smile through the darkness.

'See what the stars have done,' he said, and brought in the Astrologer's baby in his arms.

After she had nursed it against her and it had cried on the

bosom of her dress, she told him how she had feared his going.

'What should I be doing with a policeman?'

She told him that the policeman wanted her. 'What have you done for a policeman to be wanting you?'

She did not answer but took the child nearer to her wasted breast. He saw her thinness.

'You must eat, Cardiff,' he said.

Then the child began to cry. From a little wail its voice rose into a tempest of despair. The girl rocked it to and fro on her lap, but nothing soothed it.

'Stop it! Stop it!' said the Fat Man, and the tears increased. Annie smothered it in kisses, but it howled again.

'We must do something,' she said.

'Sing it a lullaby.'

She sang, but the child did not like her singing.

'There's only one thing,' said Annie, 'we must take it on the roundabouts.' With the child's arm around her neck she stumbled down the steps and ran towards the deserted fair, the Fat Man panting behind her.

She found her way through the tents and stalls into the centre of the ground where the wooden horses stood waiting, and clambered up on to a saddle. 'Start the engine,' she called out. In the distance the Fat Man could be heard cranking up the antique machine that drove the horses all the day into a wooden gallop. She heard the spasmodic humming of the engines; the boards rattled under the horses' feet. She saw the Fat Man get up by her side, pull the central lever, and climb on to the saddle of the smallest horse of all. As the roundabout started, slowly at first and slowly gaining speed, the child at the girl's breast stopped crying and clapped its hands. The night wind tore through its hair, the music jangled in its ears. Round and round the wooden horses sped, drowning the cries of the wind with the beating of their hooves.

And so the men from the caravans found them, the Fat Man and the girl in black with a baby in her arms, racing round and round on their mechanical steeds to the ever-increasing music of the organ.

THE ENEMIES

It was morning in the green acres of the Jarvis valley, and Mr Owen was picking the weeds from the edges of his garden path. A great wind pulled at his beard, the vegetable world roared under his feet. A rook had lost itself in the sky, and was making a noise to its mate; but the mate never came, and the rook flew into the west with a woe in its beak. Mr Owen, who had stood up to ease his shoulders and look at the sky, observed how dark the wings beat against the red sun. In her draughty kitchen Mrs Owen grieved over the soup. Once, in past days, the valley had housed the cattle alone; the farm-boys came down from the hills to holla at the cattle and to drive them to be milked; but no stranger set foot in the valley. Mr Owen, walking lonely through the country, had come upon it at the end of a late summer evening when the cattle were lying down still, and the stream that divided it was speaking over the pebbles. Here, thought Mr Owen, I will build a small house with one storey, in the middle of the valley, set around by a garden. And, remembering clearly the way he had come along the winding hills, he returned to his village and the questions of Mrs Owen. So it came about that a house with one storey was built in the green fields; a garden was dug and planted, and a low fence put up around the garden to keep the cows from the vegetables.

That was early in the year. Now summer and autumn had gone over; the garden had blossomed and died; there was frost at the weeds. Mr Owen bent down again, tidying the path, while the wind blew back the heads of the nearby grasses and made an oracle of each green mouth. Patiently he strangled the weeds; up came the roots, making war in the soul around them; insects were busy in the holes where the weeds had sprouted, but, dying between his fingers, they left no stain. He grew tired of their death, and tireder of the fall of the weeds. Up came the roots, down went the cheap, green heads.

Mrs Owen, peering into the depths of her crystal, had left the soup to bubble on unaided. The ball grew dark, then lightened as a rainbow moved within it. Growing hot like a sun, and cooling again like an arctic star, it shone in the folds of her dress where she held it lovingly. The tea-leaves in her cup at breakfast had told of a dark stranger. What would the crystal tell her? Mrs Owen wondered.

Up came the roots, and a crooked worm, disturbed by the probing of the fingers, wriggled blind in the sun. Of a sudden the valley filled all its hollows with the wind, with the voice of the roots, with the breathing of the nether sky. Not only a mandrake screams; torn roots have their cries; each weed Mr Owen pulled out of the ground screamed like a baby. In the village behind the hill the wind would be raging, the clothes on the garden lines would be set to strange dances. And women with shapes in their wombs would feel a new knocking as they bent over the steamy tubs. Life would go on in the veins, in the bones, the bin-ding flesh, that had their seasons and their weathers even as the valley binding the house about with the flesh of the green grass.

The ball, like an open grave, gave up its dead to Mrs Owen. She stared on the lips of women and the hairs of men that wound into a pattern on the face of the crystal world. But suddenly the patterns were swept away, and she could see nothing but the shapes of the Jarvis hills. A man with a black hat was walking down the paths into the in-visible valley beneath. If he walked any nearer he would fall into her lap. 'There's a man with a black hat walking on the hills,' she called through the window. Mr Owen smiled and went on weeding.

It was at this time that the Reverend Mr Davies lost his way; he had been losing it most of the morning, but now he had lost it altogether, and stood perturbed under a tree on the rim of the Jarvis hills. A great wind blew through

the branches, and a great grey-green earth moved un-
steadily beneath him. Wherever he looked the hills stormed
up to the sky, and wherever he sought to hide from the
wind he was frightened by the darkness. The farther he
walked, the stranger was the scenery around him; it rose
to undreamed-of heights, and then fell down again into a
valley no bigger than the palm of his hand. And the trees
walked like men. By a divine coincidence he reached the
rim of the hills just as the sun reached the centre of the sky.
With the wide world rocking from horizon to horizon, he
stood under a tree and looked down into the valley. In the
fields was a little house with a garden. The valley roared
around it, the wind leapt at it like a boxer, but the house
stood still. To Mr Davies it seemed as though the house
had been carried out of a village by a large bird and placed
in the very middle of the tumultuous universe.

But as he climbed over the craggy edges and down the
side of the hill, he lost his place in Mrs Owen's crystal. A
cloud displaced his black hat, and under the cloud walked a
very old phantom, a shape of air with stars all frozen in its
beard, and a half-moon for a smile. Mr Davies knew nothing of this as the stones scratched his hands. He was old,
he was drunk with the wine of the morning, but the stuff
that came out of his cuts was a human blood.

Nor did Mr Owen, with his face near the soil and his
hands on the necks of the screaming weeds, know of the
transformation in the crystal. He had heard Mrs Owen pro-
phesy the coming of the black hat, and had smiled as he
always smiled at her faith in the powers of darkness. He had
looked up when she called, and, smiling, had returned to
the clearer call of the ground. 'Multiply, multiply,' he had
said to the worms disturbed in their channelling, and had
cut the brown worms in half so that the halves might breed
and spread their life over the garden and go out, contami-
nating, into the fields and the bellies of the cattle.

Of this Mr Davies knew nothing. He saw a young man
with a beard bent industriously over the garden soil; he

saw that the house was a pretty picture, with the face of a pale young woman pressed up against the window. And, removing his black hat, he introduced himself as the rector of a village some ten miles away.

'You are bleeding,' said Mr Owen.

Mr Davies's hands, indeed, were covered in blood.

When Mrs Owen had seen to the rector's cuts, she sat him down in the arm-chair near the window, and made him a strong cup of tea.

'I saw you on the hill,' she said, and he asked her how she had seen him, for the hills are high and a long way off.

'I have good eyes,' she answered.

He did not doubt her. Her eyes were the strangest he had seen.

'It is quiet here,' said Mr Davies.

'We have no clock,' she said, and laid the table for three.

'You are very kind.'

'We are kind to those that come to us.'

He wondered how many came to the lonely house in the valley, but did not question her for fear of what she would reply. He guessed she was an uncanny woman loving the dark because it was dark. He was too old to question the secrets of darkness, and now, with the black suit torn and wet and his thin hands bound with the bandages of the stranger woman, he felt older than ever. The winds of the morning might blow him down, and the sudden dropping of the dark be blind in his eyes. Rain might pass through him as it passes through the body of a ghost. A tired, white-haired old man, he sat under the window, almost invisible against the panes and the white cloth of the chair.

Soon the meal was ready, and Mr Owen came in un-washed from the garden.

'Shall I say grace?' asked Mr Davies when all three were seated around the table.

Mrs Owen nodded.

'O Lord God Almighty, bless this our meal,' said Mr Davies. Looking up as he continued his prayer, he saw that

Mr and Mrs Owen had closed their eyes. 'We thank Thee for the bounties that Thou hast given us.' And he saw that the lips of Mr and Mrs Owen were moving softly. He could not hear what they said, but he knew that the prayers they spoke were not his prayers.

'Amen,' said all three together.

Mr Owen, proud in his eating, bent over the plate as he had bent over the complaining weeds. Outside the window was the brown body of the earth, the green skin of the grass, and the breasts of the Jarvis hills; there was a wind that chilled the animal earth, and a sun that had drunk up the dews on the fields; there was creation sweating out of the pores of the trees; and the grains of sand on far-away seashores would be multiplying as the sea rolled over them. He felt the coarse foods on his tongue; there was a meaning in the rind of the meat, and a purpose in the lifting of food to mouth. He saw, with a sudden satisfaction, that Mrs Owen's throat was bare.

She, too, was bent over her plate, but was letting the teeth of her fork nibble at the corners of it. She did not eat, for the old powers were upon her, and she dared not lift up her head for the greenness of her eyes. She knew by the sound which way the wind blew in the valley; she knew the stage of the sun by the curve of the shadows on the cloth. Oh, that she could take her crystal, and see within it the stretches of darkness covering up this winter light. But there was a darkness gathering in her mind, drawing in the light around her. There was a ghost on her left; with all her strength she drew in the intangible light that moved around him, and mixed it in her dark brains.

Mr Davies, like a man sucked by a bird, felt desolation in his veins, and, in a sweet delirium, told of his adventures on the hills, of how it had been cold and blowing, and how the hills went up and down. He had been lost, he said, and had found a dark retreat to shelter from the bullies in the wind; but the darkness had frightened him, and he had walked again on the hills where the morning tossed him about like a ship on the sea. Wherever he went he was blown in the open or frightened in the narrow shades. There was nowhere, he said pityingly, for an old man to go. Loving his parish, he had loved the surrounding lands, but the hills had given under his feet or plunged him into the air. And, loving his God, he had loved the darkness where men of old had worshipped the dark invisible. But now the hill caves were full of shapes and voices that mocked him because he was old.

'He is frightened of the dark,' thought Mrs Owen, 'the lovely dark.' With a smile, Mr Owen thought: 'He is frightened of the worm in the earth, of the copulation in the tree, of the living grease in the soil.' They looked at the old man, and saw that he was more ghostly than ever. The window behind him cast a ragged circle of light round his head.

Suddenly Mr Davies knelt down to pray. He did not understand the cold in his heart nor the fear that bewildered him as he knelt, but, speaking his prayers for deliverance, he stared up at the shadowed eyes of Mrs Owen and at the smiling eyes of her husband. Kneeling on the carpet at the head of the table, he stared in bewilderment at the dark mind and the gross dark body. He stared and he prayed, like an old god beset by his enemies.

CONVERSATION ABOUT
CHRISTMAS

Small Boy. Years and years and years ago, when you were a boy—

Self. When there were wolves in Wales, and birds the colour of red-flannel petticoats whisked past the harp-shaped hills, when we sang and wallowed all night and day in caves that smelt like Sunday afternoons in damp front farmhouse parlours, and chased, with the jawbones of deacons, the English and the bears—

Small Boy. You are not so old as Mr Benyon Number Twenty-Two who can remember when there were no motors. Years and years ago, when you were a boy—

Self. Oh, before the motor even, before the wheel, before the duchess-faced horse, when we rode the daft and happy hills bare-back—

Small Boy. You're not so daft as Mrs Griffiths up the street, who says she puts her ear under the water in the reservoir and listens to the fish talk Welsh. When you were a boy, what was Christmas like?

Self. It snowed.

Small Boy. It snowed last year, too. I made a snowman and my brother knocked it down and I knocked my brother down and then we had tea.

Self. But that was not the same snow. Our snow was not only shaken in whitewash buckets down the sky, I think it came shawling out of the ground and swam and drifted out of the arms and hands and bodies of the trees; snow grew overnight on the roofs of the houses like a pure and grandfather moss, minutely ivied the walls, and settled on the postman, opening the gate, like a dumb, numb thunderstorm of white torn Christmas cards.

Small Boy. Were there postmen, then, too?

Self. With sprinkling eyes and wind-cherried noses, on spread, frozen feet they crunched up to the doors and mittened on them manfully. But all that the children could hear was a ringing of bells.

Small Boy. You mean that the postman went rat-a-tat-tat and the doors rang?

Self. The bells that the children could hear were inside them.

Small Boy. I only hear thunder sometimes, never bells.

Self. There were church bells, too.

Small Boy. Inside them?

Self. No, no, no, in the bat-black, snow-white belfries, tugged by bishops and storks. And they rang their tidings over the bandaged town, over the frozen foam of the powder and ice-cream hills, over the crackling sea. It seemed that all the churches boomed, for joy, under my window; and the weather-cocks crew for Christmas, on our fence.

Small Boy. Get back to the postmen.

Self. They were just ordinary postmen, fond of walking, and dogs, and Christmas, and the snow. They knocked on the doors with blue knuckles—

Small Boy. Ours has got a black knocker—

Self. And then they stood on the white welcome mat in the little, drifted porches, and clapped their hands together, and huffed and puffed, making ghosts with their breath, and jogged from foot to foot like small boys wanting to go out.

Small Boy. And then the Presents?

Self. And then the Presents, after the Christmas box. And the cold postman, with a rose on his button-nose, tingled down the teatray-slithered run of the chilly glinting hill. He went in his ice-bound boots like a man on fishmonger's slabs. He wagged his bag like a frozen camel's hump, dizzily turned the corner on one foot, and, by God, he was gone.

Small Boy. Get back to the Presents.

Self. There were the Useful Presents: engulfing mufflers of the old coach days, and mittens made for giant sloths;

zebra scarves of a substance like silky gum that could be tug-o'-warred down to the goloshes; blinding tam-o'-shanters like patchwork tea-cosies, and bunnyscutted busbies and balaclavas for victims of head-shrinking tribes; from aunts who always wore wool-next-to-the-skin, there were moustached and rasping vests that made you wonder why the aunties had any skin left at all; and once I had a little crocheted nose-bag from an aunt now, alas, no longer whinnying with us. And pictureless books in which small boys, though warned, with quotations, not to, *would* skate on Farmer Garge's pond, and did, and drowned; and books that told me everything about the wasp, except why.

Small Boy. Get on to the Useless Presents.

Self. On Christmas Eve I hung at the foot of my bed Bessie Bunter's black stocking, and always, I said, I would stay awake all the moonlit, snowlit night to hear the roof-alighting reindeer and see the hollied boot descend through soot. But soon the sand of the snow drifted into my eyes, and, though I stared towards the fire-place and around the flickering room where the black sack-like stocking hung, I was asleep before the chimney trembled and the room was red and white with Christmas. But in the morning, though no snow melted on the bedroom floor, the stocking bulged and brimmed: press it, it squeaked like a mouse-in-a-box; it smelt of tangerine; a furry arm lolled over, like the arm of a kangaroo out of its mother's belly; squeeze it hard in the middle, and something squelched; squeeze it again – squelch again. Look out of the frost-scribbled window: on the great loneliness of the small hill, a blackbird was silent in the snow.

Small Boy. Were there any sweets?

Self. Of course there were sweets. It was the marshmallows that squelched. Hardboileds, toffee, fudge and allsorts, crunches, cracknels, humbugs, glaciers, and marzipan and butterwelsh for the Welsh. And troops of bright tin soldiers who, if they would not fight, could always run.

And Snakes-and-Families and Happy Ladders. And Easy Hobbi-Games for Little Engineers, complete with Instructions. Oh, easy for Leonardo! And a whistle to make the dogs bark to wake up the old man next door to make him beat on the wall with his stick to shake our picture off the wall. And a packet of cigarettes: you put one in your mouth and you stood at the corner of the street and you waited for hours, in vain, for an old lady to scold you for smoking a cigarette and then, with a smirk, you ate it. And, last of all, in the toe of the stocking, sixpence like a silver corn. And then downstairs for breakfast under the balloons!

Small Boy. Were there Uncles, like in our house?

Self. There are always Uncles at Christmas. The same Uncles. And on Christmas mornings, with dog-disturbing whistle and sugar fags, I would scour the swathed town for the news of the little world, and find always a dead bird by the white Bank or by the deserted swings: perhaps a robin, all but one of his fires out, and that fire still burning on his breast. Men and women wading and scooping back from church or chapel, with taproom noses and wind-smacked cheeks, all albinos, huddled their stiff black jarring feathers against the irreligious snow. Mistletoe hung from the gas in all the front parlours; there was sherry and walnuts and bottled beer and crackers by the dessert-spoons; and cats in their fur-abouts watched the fires; and the high-heaped fires crackled and spat, all ready for the chestnuts and the mulling pokers. Some few large men sat in the front parlours, without their collars. Uncles almost certainly, trying their new cigars, holding them out judiciously at arm's-length, returning them to their mouths, coughing, then holding them out again as though waiting for the explosion; and some few small aunts, not wanted in the kitchen, nor anywhere else for that matter, sat on the very edges of their chairs, poised and brittle, afraid to break, like faded cups and saucers. Not many those mornings trod the piling streets: an old man always, fawn-bowlered, yellow-gloved, and, at this time of year, with spats of snow, would take his constitutional to the white bowling-green, and back, as he would take it wet or fine on Christmas Day or Doomsday; sometimes two hale young men, with big pipes blazing, no overcoats, and windblown scarves, would trudge, unspeaking, down to the forlorn sea, to work up an appetite, to blow away the fumes, who knows, to walk into the waves until nothing of them was left but the two curling smoke clouds of their inextinguishable briars.

Small Boy. Why didn't you go home for Christmas dinner?

Self. Oh, but I did, I always did. I would be slap-dashing home, the gravy smell of the dinners of others, the bird smell, the brandy, the pudding and mince, weaving up my nostrils, when out of a snow-clogged side-lane would come a boy the spit of myself, with a pink-tipped cigarette and the violet past of a black eye, cocky as a bullfinch, leering all to himself. I hated him on sight and sound, and would be about to put my dog-whistle to my lips and blow him off the face of Christmas when suddenly he, with a violet wink, put *his* whistle to *his* lips and blew so stridently, so high, so exquisitely loud, that gobbling faces, their cheeks bulged with goose, would press against their tinselled windows, the whole length of the white echoing street.

Small Boy. What did you have for Dinner?

Self. Turkey, and blazing pudding.

Small Boy. Was it nice?

Self. It was not made on earth.

Small Boy. What did you do after dinner?

Self. The Uncles sat in front of the fire, took off their collars, loosened all buttons, put their large moist hands over their watch-chains, groaned a little, and slept. Mothers, aunts, and sisters scuttled to and fro, bearing tureens. The dog was sick. Auntie Beattie had to have three aspirins, but Auntie Hannah, who liked port, stood in the middle of the snowbound back-yard, singing like a big-bosomed thrush. I would blow up balloons to see how big they would blow up to; and, when they burst, which they all did, the Uncles jumped and rumbled. In the rich and heavy afternoon, the Uncles breathing like dolphins and the snow descending, I would sit in the front room, among festoons and Chinese lanterns, and nibble at dates, and try to make a model man-o'-war, following the Instructions for Little Engineers, and produce what might be mistaken for a sea-going tram. And then, at Christmas tea, the recovered Uncles would be jolly over their mince-pies; and the great iced cake loomed in the centre of the table like a marble grave. Auntie Hannah laced her tea with rum, because it was only once a year. And in the evening, there was Music. An uncle played the fiddle, a cousin sang 'Cherry Ripe', and another uncle sang 'Drake's Drum'. It was very warm in the little house. Auntie Hannah, who had got on to the parsnip wine, sang a song about Rejected Love, and Bleeding Hearts, and Death, and then another in which she said that her Heart was like a Bird's Nest; and then everybody laughed again, and then I went to bed. Looking through my bedroom window, out into the moonlight and the flying, unending, smoke-coloured snow, I could see the lights in the windows of all the other houses on our hill, and hear the music rising from them up the long, steadily falling night. I turned the gas down, I got into bed. I said some words to the close and holy darkness, and then I slept.

Small Boy. But it all sounds like an ordinary Christmas.

Self. It was.

Small Boy. But Christmas when you were a boy wasn't any different to Christmas now.

Self. It was, it was.

Small Boy. Why was Christmas different then?

Self. I mustn't tell you.

Small Boy. Why mustn't you tell me? Why is Christmas different for me?

Self. I mustn't tell you.

Small Boy. Why can't Christmas be the same for me as it was for you when you were a boy?

Self. I mustn't tell you. I mustn't tell you because it is Christmas now.

HOW TO BE A POET

An Editor, in a moment of over-confidence, has invited me to talk about this subject.

Imagine all other subjects he might have suggested: The Development of the Seduction Scene in Watts-Dunton; Charles Morgan, my favourite character in fiction; Mr T. S. Eliot and the Dollar Crisis; The Influence of Laurel and Hardy and Laurel on Hardy. As Fowler, of English Usage puts it: 'What words could not one use were those subjects but to be dealt with and referred to.' But, like a contrary cobbler, I must stick to my first.

Let me, at once, make it clear that I am not considering, in the supposedly informative jottings, Poetry as an Art or Craft, as the rhythmic verbal expression of a spiritual necessity or urge, but solely as the means to a social end; that end being the achievement of a status in society solid enough to warrant the poet discarding and expunging those affectations, so essential in the early stages, of speech, dress, and behaviour; an income large enough to satisfy his physical demands, unless he has already fallen victim to the Poet's Evil, or Great Wen; and a permanent security from the fear of having to write any more. I do not intend to ask, let alone to answer, the question: 'Is Poetry a Good Thing?' but only: 'Can Poetry be made Good Business?'

I shall, to begin with, introduce to you, with such comments as may or may not be necessary, a few of the main types of poets who have made the social and financial grade.

First, though not in order of importance, is the poet who has emerged docketed 'lyrical', from the Civil Service. He can be divided, so far as his physical appearance goes, into two types. He is either thin, not to say of a shagged-out appearance, with lips as fulsome, sensual, and inviting as a hen's ovipositor, bald from all too masculate birth, his eyes made small and reddened by reading books in French, a language he cannot understand, in an attic in the provinces while young and repellent, his voice like the noise of a mouse's nail on tinfoil, his nostrils transparent, his breath grey; or else he is jowled and bushy, with curved pipe and his nose full of dottle, the look of all Sussex in his stingo'd eyes, his burry tweeds smelling of the dogs he loathes, with a voice like a literate Airedale's that has learnt its vowels by correspondence course, and an intimate friend of Chesterton's, whom he never met.

Let us see in what manner our man has arrived at his present and enviable position as the Poet who has made Poetry Pay.

Dropped into the Civil Service at an age when many of our young poets now are running away to Broadcasting House, to-day's equivalent of the Sea, he is at first lost to sight in the mountains of red tape which, in future years, he is so mordantly, though with a wry and puckered smile, to dismiss in a paragraph in his 'Around and About My Shelves'. After a few years, he begins to peer out from the forms and files in which he leads his ordered, nibbling life, and picks up a cheese crumb here, a dropping there, in his ink-stained thumbs. His ears are uncannily sensitive: he can hear an opening being opened a block of offices away. And soon he learns that a poem in a Civil Service magazine is, if not a step up the ladder, at least a lick in the right direction. And he writes a poem. It is, of course, about Nature; it confesses a wish to escape from humdrum routine and embrace the unsophisticated life of the farm labourer; he desires, though without scandal, to wake up with the birds; he expresses the opinion that a ploughshare, not a pen, best fits his little strength: a decorous pantheist, he is one with the rill, the rhyming mill, the rosy-bottomed milkmaid, the russet-cheeked rat-catcher, swains, swine, pipits, pippins. You can smell the country in his poems, the fields, the flowers, the armpits of Triptolemus, the barns, the pyres, the hay, and, most of all, the corn. The poem is

published. A single lyrical extract from the beginning must
suffice:

> The roaring street is hushed!
> Hushed, do I say?
> The wing of a bird has brushed
> Time's cobwebs away.
> Still, still as death, the air
> over the grey stones!
> And over the grey thoroughfare
> I hear – sweet tones!
> A blackbird open its bill,
> – A blackbird, aye! –
> And sing its liquid fill
> From the London sky.

A little time after the publication of the poem, he is nodded
to in the corridor by Hotchkiss of Inland Revenue, himself
a week-ending poet with two slim volumes to his credit,
half an inch in the Poet's Who's Who or the Newbolt
Calendar, an ambitious wife with a vee-neck and a fringe
who lost the battle of the Slade, a small car that always
drives, as though by itself, to Sussex – as a parson's horse
would once unthinkingly trot to the public house – and an
unfinished monograph on the influence of Blunden on the
hedgerow.

Hotchkiss, lunching with Sowerby of Customs, himself
a literary figure of importance with a weekly column in
Will o' Lincoln's Weekly and his name on the editorial list of
the Masterpiece of the Fortnight Club (volumes at reduced
rates to all writers, and a complete set of the works of Mary
Webb quarter-price at Christmas), says casually: 'You've
rather a promising fellow in your department, Sowerby.
Young Cribbe. I've been reading a little thing of his, "I
desire the Curlew".' And Cribbe's name goes the small,
foetid rounds.

He is next asked to contribute a *group* of poems to Hotchkiss's anthology, 'New Pipes', which Sowerby praises – 'A

rare gift for the haunting phrase' – in *Will o' Lincoln's*.
Cribbe sends copies of the anthology, each laboriously
signed: 'To the greatest living English poet, in homage,' to
twenty of the dullest poets still on their hind legs. Some
of his inscribed gifts are acknowledged. Sir Tom Knight
spares a few generous, though bemused, moments to
scribble a message on a sheet of crested writing-paper re-
moved, during a never-to-be-repeated week-end visit, from
a short-sighted, but not all that short-sighted peer. 'Dear
Mr Crabbe,' Sir Tom writes, 'I appreciate your little tri-
bute. Your poem, "Nocturne with Lilies", is worthy of
Shanks. Go on. Go on. There is room on the mount.' The
fact that Cribbe's poem is not 'Nocturne with Lilies' at all,
but 'On Hearing Delius by a Lych-Gate', does not perturb
Cribbe, who carefully files the letter, after blowing away
the dandruff, and soon is in the throes of collecting his
poems together to make, *misericordia*, a book, 'Linnet and
Spindle', dedicated 'to Clem Sowerby, that green-fingered
gardener in the Gardens of the Hesperides.'

The book appears. Some favourable notice is taken, parti-
cularly in Middlesex. And Sowerby, too modest to review
it himself after such a gratifying dedication, reviews it
under a different name. 'This young poet,' he writes, 'is not,
thanks be it, too "modernistic" to pay reverence to the
shining source of his inspiration. Cribbe will go far.'

And Cribbe goes to his publishers. A contract is drawn
up, Messrs Stitch & Time undertake to publish his next
book of verse on condition that they have the option on his
next nine novels. He contrives also to be engaged as a
casual reader of manuscripts to Messrs Stitch & Time, and
returns home clutching a parcel which contains a book on
the *Development of the Oxford Movement in Finland* by a Cots-
wold Major, three blank-verse tragedies about Mary Queen
of Scots, and a novel entitled *To-morrow, Jennifer*.

Now Cribbe, until his contract, has never thought of
writing a novel. But undaunted by the fact that he cannot

tell one person from another – people, to him, are all one dull, grey mass, except celebrities and departmental superiors – that he has no interest whatsoever in anything they do or say, except in so far as it concerns his career, and that his inventive resources are as limited as those of a chipmunk on a treadmill, he sits down in his shirt-sleeves, loosens his collar, thumbs in the shag, and begins to study in earnest how best, with no qualifications, to make a success of commercial fiction. He soon comes to the conclusion that only quick sales and ephemeral reputations are made by tough novels with such titles as *I've Got It Coming* or *Ten Cents a Dice*; by proletarian novels about the conversion to dialectical materialism of Palais-de wide boys, entitled, maybe, *Red Rain on You, Alf*; by novels called maybe, *Melody in Clover*, about dark men with slight limps, called Dirk Conway and their love for two women, lascivious Ursula Mountclare and little, shy Fay Waters. And he soon sees that only the smallest sales, and notices only in the loftiest monthlies of the most limited circulation, will ever result from his writing such a novel as *The Inner Zodiac*, by G. H. Q. Bidet, a ruthless analysis of the idealogical conflicts arising from the relationship between Philip Armour, an international impotent physicist, Tristram Wolf, a bisexual sculptor in teak, and Philip's virginal but dynamic Creole wife, Titania, a lecturer in Balkan Economics, and how these highly sensitized characters – so redolent, as they are, of the post-Sartre Age – react a profound synthesis while working together, for the sake of One-ness, in a Unesco Clinic.

No fool, Cribbe realizes, even in the early stages of exploration, with theodolite and respirator through darkest Foyle, that the novel to write is that which commands a steady, unsensational, provincial, and suburban sale and concerns, for choice, the birth, education, financial ups-and-downs, marriages, separations, and deaths of five generations of a family of Lancashire cotton-brokers. This novel, he grasps at once, should be in the form of a trilogy, and each volume should bear some such solid, uneventful title as *The Warp*, *The Woof*, and *The Way*. And he sets to work. From the reviews of Cribbe's first novel, one may select: 'Here is sound craftsmanship allied to sterling characterization.' 'Incidents a-plenty.' 'You become as familiar with George Steadiman, his wife Muriel, old Tobias Matlock (a delightful vignette) and all the inhabitants of Loom House, as you do with your own family.' 'These dour Northcotes grow on you.' 'English as Manchester rain.' 'Mr Cribbe is a bull-terrier.' 'A story in the Phyllis Bottome class.' On the success of the novel, Cribbe joins the N.I.B. Club, delivers a paper on the Early Brett Young Country, and becomes a regular reviewer praising every other novel he receives – ('The prose shimmers') – and inviting every third novelist to dine at the Servile Club, to which he has recently been elected.

When the whole of the trilogy has appeared, Cribbe rises, like scum, to the N.I.B. committee, attends all the memorial services for men of letters who are really dead for the first time in fifty years, tears up his old contract and signs another, brings out a new novel, which becomes a Book Society choice, is offered, by Messrs Stitch & Time, a position in an 'advisory capacity', which he accepts, leaves the Civil Service, buys a cottage in Bucks ('You wouldn't think it was only thirty miles from London, would you? Look, old man, see that crested grebe.' A starling flies by), a new secretary whom he later marries for her touch-typing. Poetry? Perhaps a sonnet in the *Sunday Times* every now and then; a little collection of verse once in a while ('My first love, you know'). But it doesn't really bother him any more, though it got him where he is. *He has made the grade!*

And now we must move to see for a moment a very different kind of poet, whom we shall call Cedric. To follow in Cedric's footsteps – (he'd love you to, and would never call a policeman unless it was that frightfully sinister sergeant you see sometimes in Mecklenburgh Square, just like an El Greco) – you must be born twilightly into the middle classes, or go to one of the correct schools – (which, of course, you must loathe, for it is essential, from the first, to be misunderstood) – and arrive at the University with your reputation already established as a coming poet and looking, if possible, something between a Guards' officer and a fashionable photographer's doxy. You may say: But how is one to arrive with one's reputation already established as 'a poet to watch'? (Poet-watching may in future become as popular as bird-watching. And it is quite reasonable to imagine the editorial offices of *The Poetaster* being bought up by the nation as a sanctuary.) But that is a question outside the scope of these all-too-rough notes, as it must be assumed that anyone wishing to take up Poetry as a career has always known how to turn the stuff out when required. And also Cedric's college tutor was his housemaster's best friend. So here is Cedric, known already to the discerning few for his sensitive poems about golden limbs, sun-jewelled fronds, the ambrosia of the first shy kiss in the delicate-traceried caverns of the moon (really the school boot-cupboard), at the threshold of fame and the world laid out before him like a row of balletomanes.

If this were the twenties, Cedric's first book of poems, published while he was still an undergraduate, might be called 'Asps and Lutes'. It would be nostalgic for a life that never was. It would be world-weary. (He once saw the world out of a train carriage window: it looked unreal.) It would be a carefully garish mixture, a cunningly evocative pudding full of plums pulled from the Sitwells and Sache-verell other people, a mildly cacophonous hothouse of exotic horticultural and comic-erotic bric-à-brac, from which I extract these typical lines:

A cornucopia of phalluses
Cascade on the vermilion palaces
In arabesques and syrup rigadoons;

> Quince-breasted Circes of the zenanas
> Do catch this rain of cherry-wigged bananas
> And saraband beneath the raspberry moons.

After a tiff with the University authorities he vanished into the Key of Blue – a made man.

If it were in the thirties, the title of his book might well be *Pharos, I warn*, and would consist of one of two kinds of verse. Either it would be made of long, lax, lackadaisical rhythms, dying falls, and images of social awareness:

> After the incessant means-test of the conspiratorial winter
> Scrutinizing the tragic history of each robbed branch,
> Look! the triumphant bourgeoning! spring gay as a
>   workers' procession
> To the newly-opened gymnasium
> Look! the full employment of the blossoms!

Or it would be daringly full of slang and street phrases, snippets of song hits, Kipling jingles, kippered blues:

> We're sitting pretty
> In the appalling city –
> I know where we're going but I don't know where from –
> Take it from me, boy,
> You're my cup-of-tea, boy,
> We're sitting on a big black bomb.

Social awareness! That was the motto. He would talk over coffee – ('Adrian makes the best coffee in the whole of this uncivilized island.' 'Tell me, Rodney, where *do* you get these delicious pink cakes?' 'It's a secret!' 'Oh, *do* tell. And I'll give you that special receipt that Basil's Colonel brought back from Ceylon, it takes three pounds of butter and a mango pod') – of spending the long vacation in 'somewhere *really* alive. I mean, but really. Like the Rhondda Valley or something. I mean, I know I'll feel really *orientated* there. I mean, one's so stagnant here. Books, books. It's people that count. I mean, one's got to know the miners.' And he spends the long vacation with Reggie, in Bonn. A volume of politico-travel chat follows, the promise of which is amply fulfilled when, years later, he turns up as Literary Secretary of I.A.C.T. (International Arts Council To-morrow).

If Cedric were writing in the forties, he would, perhaps, be engulfed, so that he could not see the wool for the Treece, in a kind of 'apocalyptic' batter, and his first Volume might be entitled *Plangent Macrocosm*, or *Heliogabalus in Pentecost*. Cedric can mix his metaphor, bog his cliché, and soak his stolen symbols in stale ass's milk as glibly and glueily as the best of them.

Next, London and the reviewing. Reviewing, obviously, the work of other poets. This, to do badly, is simple; and, though not at once, financially rewarding. The vocabulary that a conscientiously dishonest reviewer of contemporary verse must learn is limited. Trend, of course, and impact, impasto, awareness, *zeitgeist*, sphere of influence, Audenesque, the latter Yeats, period of transition, constructivism, schematic, ingeniously sprinkled, will help along, no end, the short and sweeping dismissal of the life-work of any adult and responsible poet. The principal rules are few to remember: when reviewing, say, two entirely dis-similar books of verse, pit one against the other as though they were originally written in a strict competition. 'After Mr A's subtle, taut, and integrated poetical comments or near-epigrams, Mr B's long and sonorous heroic narrative, for all its textural richness and vibrative orchestration, rings curiously hollow' is an example of this most worth-while and labour-saving device. Decide, quite carefully, to be a staunch admirer of one particular poet, whether you like his poetry or not; cash in on him; make him your own; patent him; carve a niche with him. Bring his name, gratuitously, into your reviews: 'Mr E is, unfortunately, a poet much given to rhodomontade (unlike Hector Whistle).' 'Reading Mr D's admirable scholarly though, in places, pedestrian translations, we find ourselves longing for the cool ardour and consummate craftsmanship of Hector Whistle.' Be careful when you choose your poet, not to poach. Ask yourself first: 'Is Hector Whistle anyone else's pigeon?'

Read all other reviews of the books you are about to review before you say a word yourself. Quote from the poems only when pressed for time; a review should be about the reviewer, not the poet. Be careful not to slate a bad rich poet unless he is notoriously mean, dead, or in America, for it is not such a long step from reviewing verse to editing a magazine, and the rich bad poet may well put up the money.

Returning to Cedric, let us suppose that he has, as a result of comparing a rich young man's verse with Auden's to the detriment of Auden's, been given the editorship of a new literary periodical. (He may also be given a flat. If not, he should insist that the new periodical must have commodious offices. He then lives in them.) Cedric's first problem is what to call the thing. This is not easy, as most of the names that mean nothing at all – essential to the success of the new project – have all been used: *Horizon, Polemic, Harvest, Caravel, Seed, Transition, Kingdom Come, Focus, View, Accent, Apocalypse, Arena, Circus, Cronos, Signposts, Wind and Rain* – they've all been had. Can you hear Cedric's mind churning away? 'Vacuum,' 'Volcano,' 'Limbo,' 'Milestone,' 'Need,' 'Eruption,' 'Uterus,' 'Seismograph,' 'Vulcan,' 'Cognizance,' 'Schism,' 'Data,' 'Arson.' Yes, he's got it: 'Chiaroscuro.' And the rest is easy : just editing.

But let us look, very quickly, at some other methods of making poetry a going concern.

The Provincial Rush, or the Up-Rimbaud-and-At-'Em approach. This is not wholeheartedly to be recommended as certain qualifications are essential. Before you swoop and burst upon the centre of literary activity – which means, when you are very young, the right pubs, and, later the right flats, and later still, the right clubs – you must have behind you a body (it need have no head) of ferocious and un-understandable verse. (It is not, as I said before, my function to describe how these *gauche* and verbose ecstasies are achieved. Hart Crane found that, while listening, drunk, to Sibelius, he could turn out the stuff like billiho. A friend of mine, who has been suffering from a violent headache since he was eight, finds it so easy to write anyway, he has to tie knots in his handkerchief to remind him to stop. There are many methods, and always, when there's a will and slight delirium, there's a way.) And again, this poet must possess a thirst and constitution like that of a salt-eating pony, a hippo's hide, boundless energy, prodigious conceit, no scruples, and – most important of all, this can never be over-estimated – a home to go *back* to in the provinces whenever he breaks down.

I'm afraid I must go very rapidly through a few of the other classifications.

Of the poet who merely writes because he wants to write, who does not deeply mind if he is published or not, and who can put up with poverty and total lack of recognition in his lifetime, nothing of any pertinent value can be said. He is no business man. Posterity Does Not Pay.

Also, and highly *un*recommended, are the following:

The writing of limericks. Vast market, little or no pay.
Poems in crackers. Too seasonal.
Poems for children. This will kill you and the children.
Obituaries in verse. Only established favourites used.
Poetry as a method of blackmail (by boring). Dangerous. The one you blackmail might retaliate by reading you aloud his unfinished tragedy about St Bernard: 'The Flask'.

And lastly: *Poems on lavatory walls.* The reward is purely psychological.

Thank you.